Fact File

A Marine Mammal

Sea Otter

habitat range

Sea otters weigh as much as 65 pounds and they stay in the cold ocean water almost all the time.

Sea otters wrap themselves in seaweed, which keeps them from drifting when they sleep.

HOUGHTON MIFFLIN

California Science

 HOUGHTON MIFFLIN   BOSTON

Program Authors

William Badders
Director of the Cleveland Mathematics and
Science Partnership
Cleveland Municipal School District, Cleveland, Ohio

Douglas Carnine, Ph.D.
Professor of Education
University of Oregon, Eugene, Oregon

James Feliciani
Supervisor of Instructional Media and Technology
Land O' Lakes, Florida

Bobby Jeanpierre, Ph.D.
Assistant Professor, Science Education
University of Central Florida, Orlando, Florida

Carolyn Sumners, Ph.D.
Director of Astronomy and Physical Sciences
Houston Museum of Natural Science, Houston, Texas

Catherine Valentino
Author-in-Residence
Houghton Mifflin, West Kingston, Rhode Island

Primary Grade Consultant

Kathleen B. Horstmeyer
Past President SEPA
Carefree, Arizona

Content Consultants

See Teacher's Edition for a complete list.

California Teacher Reviewers

Robert Aikman
Cunningham Elementary
Turlock, California

Christine Anderson
Rock Creek Elementary
Rocklin, California

Dan M. Anthony
Berry Elementary
San Diego, California

Patricia Babb
Cypress Elementary
Tulare, California

Ann Balfour
Lang Ranch Elementary
Thousand Oaks, California

Colleen Briner-Schmidt
Conejo Elementary
Thousand Oaks, California

Mary Brouse
Panama Buena Vista Union
School District
Bakersfield, California

Monica Carabay
Four Creeks Elementary
Visalia, California

Printed in the U.S.A.

ISBN-13: 978-0-618-68615-5
ISBN-10: 0-618-68615-0

Science Content Standards for California Public Schools reproduced by permission, California Department of Education, CDE Press, 1430 N Street, Suite 3207, Sacramento, CA 95814.

2 3 4 5 6 7 8 9-DW-15 14 13 12 11 10 09 08 07

California Teacher Reviewers (cont'd.)

Sheri Chu
Vineyard Elementary
Ontario, California

Teena Collins
Frank D. Parent Elementary
Inglewood, California

Gary Comstock
Cole Elementary
Clovis, California

Jenny Dickinson
Bijou Community School
South Lake Tahoe, California

Cheryl Dultz
Kingswood Elementary
Citrus Heights, California

Tom East
Mountain View Elementary
Fresno, California

Sharon Ferguson
Fort Washington Elementary
Fresno, California

Robbin Ferrell
Hawthorne Elementary
Ontario, California

Mike Freedman
Alta-Dutch Flat Elementary
Alta, California

Linda Gadis-Honaker
Banyan Elementary
Alta Loma, California

Lisa Gomez
Marshall James Elementary
Modesto, California

Lisa Green
Jordan Elementary
Orange, California

Carey Iannuzzo
Fitzgerald Elementary
Rialto, California

Teresa Lorentz
Banta Elementary
Tracy, California

Christine Luellig
Henderson Elementary
Barstow, California

Peggy MacArthur
Montevideo Elementary
San Ramon, California

Jeffrey McPherson
Parkview Elementary
Garden Grove, California

Susan Moore
Lang Ranch Elementary
Thousand Oaks, California

William Neddersen
Tustin Unified School District
Tustin, California

Josette Perrie
Plaza Vista School
Irvine, California

Lisa Pulliam
Alcott Elementary
Pomona, California

Jennifer Ramirez
Skyline North Elementary
Barstow, California

Nancy Scali
Arroyo Elementary
Ontario, California

Janet Sugimoto
Sunset Lane School
Fullerton, California

Laura Valencia
Kingsley Elementary
Montclair, California

Sally Van Wagner
Antelope Creek Elementary
Rocklin, California

Jenny Wade
Stockton Unified School District
Stockton, California

Judy Williams
Price Elementary
Anaheim, California

Karen Yamamoto
Westmore Oaks Elementary
West Sacramento, California

Contents

UNIT A
Needs of Living Things

Big Idea Plants and animals meet their needs in different ways.

California poppies

California

Activities

Black bear

Contents

California

Activities

California sea lion

Contents

UNIT C
Weather Patterns

Big Idea Weather can be observed, measured, and described.

Activities

Borrego Springs, California

Contents

UNIT D
Materials and Their Forms

Big Idea Materials come in different forms (states), including solids, liquids, and gases.

Watts Towers

California

Activities

Using Your Book

The Nature of Science

Science is an adventure. People all over the world do science. You can do science, too. You probably already do.

The Nature of Science

In the front of your book you will learn about how people explore science.

Every unit in your book has two or more chapters.

You can read these on your own.

Big Idea! tells you the part of your **California Science Standards** that connects the ideas of each lesson.

LIFE **A** SCIENCE

Needs of Living Things

California valley quails

Big Idea!
Standard Set 2.
Life Sciences

Plants and animals meet their needs in different ways.

1

Lesson Preview gives information and asks questions about each lesson.

My Journal tells you to write or draw answers to the questions.

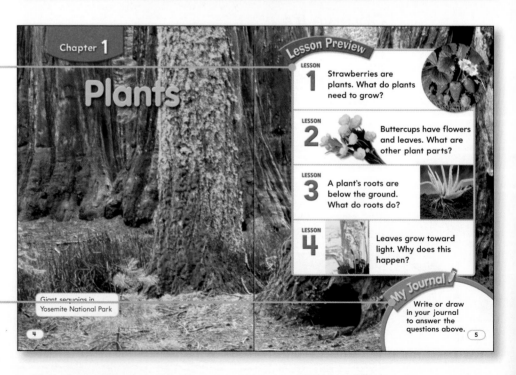

Chapter **1**

Plants

Giant sequoias in Yosemite National Park

4

Lesson Preview

LESSON **1** Strawberries are plants. What do plants need to grow?

LESSON **2** Buttercups have flowers and leaves. What are other plant parts?

LESSON **3** A plant's roots are below the ground. What do roots do?

LESSON **4** Leaves grow toward light. Why does this happen?

My Journal
Write or draw in your journal to answer the questions above.

5

Vocabulary Preview

Introduces important science terms, with pictures, and vocabulary skills.

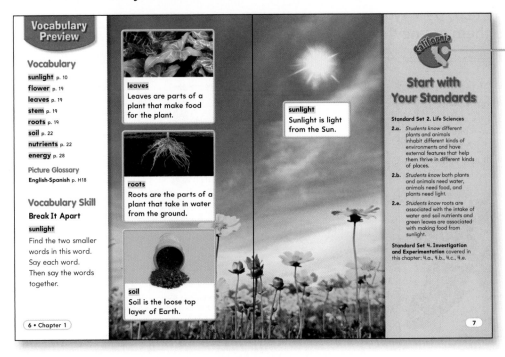

California Science Standards are identified for each chapter.

Every lesson in your book has two parts.

Part 1: Directed Inquiry

Building Background gives you science facts needed for the lessons.

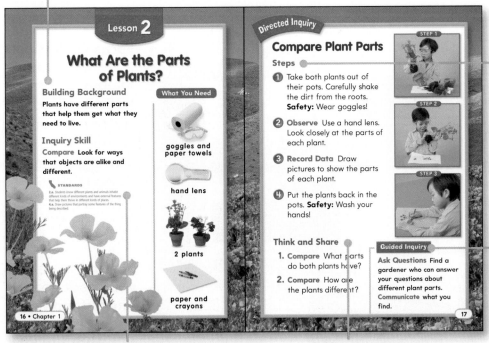

Steps to follow for the Directed Inquiry activity.

Guided Inquiry lets you do more on your own.

California Science Standards appear in blue throughout each lesson.

Think and Share lets you check what you have learned.

Part 2: Learn by Reading

Vocabulary lists the new science words you will learn. In the text, dark words with yellow around them are new words.

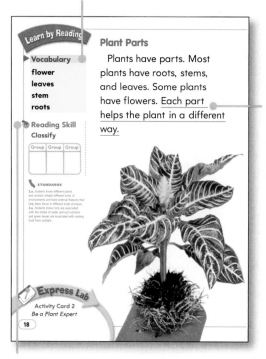

Learn by Reading

Vocabulary
flower
leaves
stem
roots

Reading Skill
Classify

Group	Group	Group

STANDARDS
2.a. Students know different plants and animals inhabit different kinds of environments and have external features that help them thrive in different kinds of places.
2.a. Students know roots are associated with the intake of water and soil nutrients and green leaves are associated with making food from sunlight.

Plant Parts

Plants have parts. Most plants have roots, stems, and leaves. Some plants have flowers. <u>Each part helps the plant in a different way.</u>

Express Lab
Activity Card 2
Be a Plant Expert

18

Main Idea is underlined to show you what is important.

Reading Skill helps you understand the text.

Lesson Wrap-Up

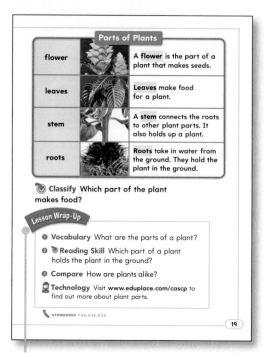

Parts of Plants

flower		A **flower** is the part of a plant that makes seeds.
leaves		**Leaves** make food for a plant.
stem		A **stem** connects the roots to other plant parts. It also holds up a plant.
roots		**Roots** take in water from the ground. They hold the plant in the ground.

Classify Which part of the plant makes food?

Lesson Wrap-Up

❶ **Vocabulary** What are the parts of a plant?

❷ **Reading Skill** Which part of a plant holds the plant in the ground?

❸ **Compare** How are plants alike?

❹ **Technology** Visit www.eduplace.com/cascp to find out more about plant parts.

STANDARDS 1:2.a, 2:2.a, 3:2.a.

19

After you read, check what you have learned.

Focus On

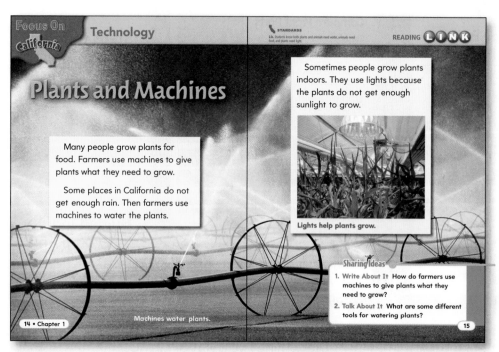

Focus On California

Technology

STANDARDS
2.b. Students know both plants and animals need water, animals need food, and plants need light.

READING **LINK**

Plants and Machines

Many people grow plants for food. Farmers use machines to give plants what they need to grow.

Some places in California do not get enough rain. Then farmers use machines to water the plants.

Sometimes people grow plants indoors. They use lights because the plants do not get enough sunlight to grow.

Lights help plants grow.

Sharing Ideas

1. **Write About It** How do farmers use machines to give plants what they need to grow?

2. **Talk About It** What are some different tools for watering plants?

14 • Chapter 1

Machines water plants.

15

Focus On lets you learn more about an important topic. Look for History of Science, Technology, Literature, Readers' Theater– and more.

Sharing Ideas has you check your understanding and write and talk about what you have learned.

Extreme Science

Compares and contrasts interesting science information.

My Journal provides a chance to write your ideas about the Extreme Science lessons.

Links and Careers/People in Science

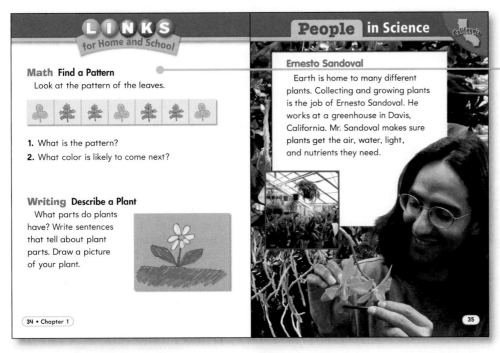

You can do these at school or at home.

Links connects science to other subject areas.

Careers/People in Science tells you about the work of a real scientist.

Review and Unit Practice

These reviews help you to know you are on track with learning California science standards.

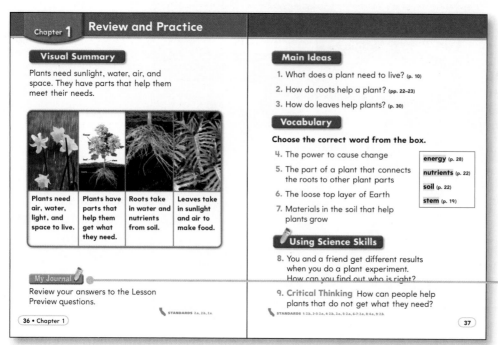

Chapter 1 **Review and Practice**

Visual Summary

Plants need sunlight, water, air, and space. They have parts that help them meet their needs.

| Plants need air, water, light, and space to live. | Plants have parts that help them get what they need. | Roots take in water and nutrients from soil. | Leaves take in sunlight and air to make food. |

My Journal
Review your answers to the Lesson Preview questions.

STANDARDS 2a, 2b, 2a

36 • Chapter 1

Main Ideas

1. What does a plant need to live? (p. 10)
2. How do roots help a plant? (pp. 22–23)
3. How do leaves help plants? (p. 30)

Vocabulary

Choose the correct word from the box.

4. The power to cause change
5. The part of a plant that connects the roots to other plant parts
6. The loose top layer of Earth
7. Materials in the soil that help plants grow

| energy (p. 28) |
| nutrients (p. 22) |
| soil (p. 22) |
| stem (p. 19) |

Using Science Skills

8. You and a friend get different results when you do a plant experiment. How can you find out who is right?
9. **Critical Thinking** How can people help plants that do not get what they need?

STANDARDS 1: 2b, 2-3: 2a, 4: 2b, 2a, 5: 2a, 6-7: 2a, 8: 4a, 9: 2b

37

My Journal tells you to review the questions you answered at the start of the chapter.

Unit Wrap-Up

Wrap-Up

You Can...

Discover More

What bird flaps its wings the fastest?

A hummingbird flaps its wings about 75 times every second! The wings move so fast that they make a humming sound. Hummingbirds are called nature's helicopters because of the way they move.

Simulations Go to www.eduplace.com/cascp to learn more about the parts of a hummingbird.

72 • Unit A

Learn more about science using the **Discover More** question.

References

Index

A

Picture Glossary

English-Spanish

Health and Fitness Handbook

Science and Math Toolbox

Science and Math Toolbox

Using a Hand Lens.......... H2
Using a Thermometer....... H3
Using a Ruler.............. H4
Using a Calculator........ H5
Using a Balance........... H6
Making a Chart........... H7
Making a Tally Chart...... H8
Making a Bar Graph...... H9

H1

The back of your book includes sections you will refer to again and again.

Start with Your Standards

Your California Science Standards

Your California Science Standards

Welcome to the adventure of science!

Many famous scientists and inventors have lived and worked in California. You could be one, too!

Your science standards tell you what you should know by the end of Grade 1. They also tell what you should be able to do when you investigate and experiment. You will find the standards printed next to each section of the lesson and chapter.

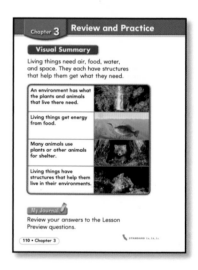

Houghton Mifflin Science will lead you to mastering your standards. Along the way, you will ask questions, do hands-on investigations, think critically, and read what scientists have discovered about how the world works. You will also get to know real people who do science every day.

How Families Can Help

- Get to know the California Science Content Standards on the pages that follow. If you want to learn more about science education, you can find the Science Framework for California Public Schools online at **www.cde.ca.gov/ci/**

- Relate the science of the standards to activities at home such as cooking, gardening, and playing sports.

- Get to know your child's science textbook, encouraging him or her to use the table of contents, index, and glossary. Point out the importance of titles and headings as a means to finding the information needed.

- Help your child choose library books to read about science, nature, inventors, and scientists. You can use the Recommended Literature for Math & Science online database at **www.cde.ca.gov/ci/sc/ll/**

- Find opportunities for your child to use numbers and mathematics skills and to measure and to estimate measurements, such as when planning a trip.

- Encourage your child to do experiments and enter science fairs.

Science Content Standards

These Science Content Standards are learning goals that you will achieve by the end of first grade. Below each standard is the unit or chapter in this book where that standard is taught. In that unit and chapter, there are many opportunities to master the standard—by doing investigations, reading, writing, speaking, and drawing concept maps.

Physical Sciences

Materials come in different forms (states), including solids, liquids, and gases. As a basis for understanding this concept:
Unit D: Materials and Their Forms

1.a. *Students know* solids, liquids, and gases have different properties.
Chapter 7: Solids, Liquids, and Gases
Chapter 8: Changes in Materials

1.b. *Students know* the properties of substances can change when the substances are mixed, cooled, or heated.
Chapter 8: Changes in Materials

Life Sciences

Set 2

Plants and animals meet their needs in different ways. As a basis of understanding this concept:

Unit A: Needs of Living Things
Unit B: Where Plants and Animals Live

2.a. *Students know* different plants and animals inhabit different kinds of environments and have external features that help them thrive in different kinds of places.

Chapter 1: Plants
Chapter 2: Animals
Chapter 3: Living Things Meet Their Needs
Chapter 4: Kinds of Environments

2.b. *Students know* both plants and animals need water, animals need food, and plants need light.

Chapter 1: Plants
Chapter 2: Animals
Chapter 3: Living Things Meet Their Needs

Channel Islands

2.c. *Students know* animals eat plants or other animals for food and may also use plants or even other animals for shelter and nesting.

2.d. *Students know* how to infer what animals eat from the shape of their teeth (e.g., sharp teeth: eats meat; flat teeth: eats plants).

2.e. *Students know* roots are associated with the intake of water and soil nutrients and green leaves are associated with making food from sunlight.

Bighorn sheep
at Mono Lake

Set 3 **Earth Sciences**

Weather can be observed, measured, and described. As a basis for understanding this concept:

Unit C: Weather Patterns

3.a. *Students know* how to use simple tools (e.g., thermometer, wind vane) to measure weather conditions and record changes from day to day and across the seasons.
Chapter 5: Weather
Chapter 6: Seasons

3.b. *Students know* that the weather changes from day to day but that trends in temperature or rain (or snow) tend to be predictable during a season.
Chapter 5: Weather
Chapter 6: Seasons

3.c. *Students know* the sun warms the land, air, and water.
Chapter 5: Weather
Chapter 6: Seasons

Investigation and Experimentation

Scientific progress is made by asking meaningful questions and conducting careful investigations. As a basis for understanding this concept and addressing the content in the other three strands, students should develop their own questions and perform investigations. Students will:

Directed Inquiry and Guided Inquiry investigations in every lesson

4.a. Draw pictures that portray features of the thing being described.

Directed Inquiry and Guided Inquiry investigations

4.b. Record observations and data with pictures, numbers, or written statements.

Directed Inquiry and Guided Inquiry investigations

4.c. Record observations on a bar graph.

Directed Inquiry and Guided Inquiry investigations

4.d. Describe the relative position by using two references (e.g., above and next to, below and left of).

Directed Inquiry and Guided Inquiry investigations

4.e. Make new observations when discrepancies exist between two descriptions of the same object or phenomenon.

Directed Inquiry and Guided Inquiry investigations

The Nature of Science

California

Science is an adventure.
People all over the world do
science. You can do science, too.
You probably already do.

Big Idea

Scientific progress is made by asking meaningful questions and conducting careful investigations.

Start With Your Standards

STANDARD SET 4. Investigation and Experimentation

4. Scientific progress is made by asking meaningful questions and conducting careful investigations. As a basis for understanding this concept and addressing the content in the other three strands, students should develop their own questions and perform investigations. Students will:

4.a. Draw pictures that portray some features of the thing being described.

4.b. Record observations and data with pictures, numbers, or written statements.

4.c. Record observations on a bar graph.

4.d. Describe the relative position of objects by using two references (e.g., above and next to, below and left of).

4.e. Make new observations when discrepancies exist between two descriptions of the same object or phenomenon.

The Nature of Science

Do What Scientists Do

Donna House planned this wetland and woods. Ms. House is a scientist. She studies plants and how native people use them. She protects plants that are in danger of dying out.

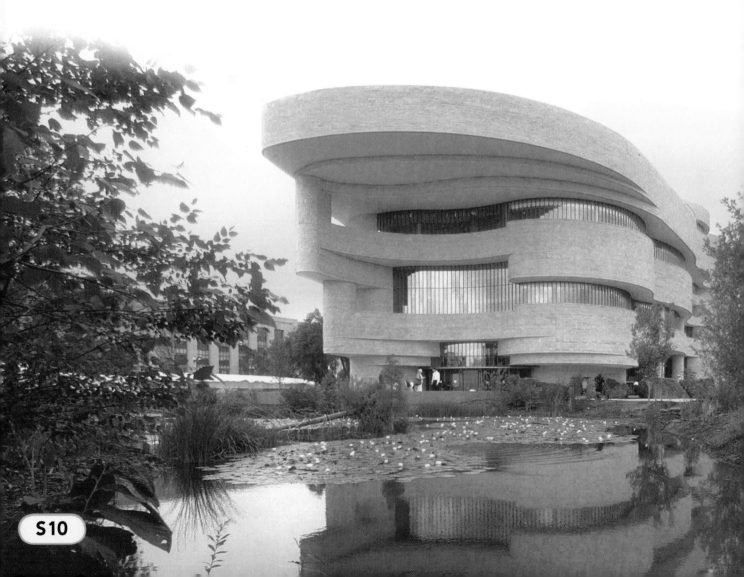

Donna House chose the wild plants around the National Museum of the American Indian in Washington, D.C.

Scientists Investigate

Scientists ask questions. They answer them by observing and testing. Donna House gathers facts about plants. She reads about plants. She uses tools to measure plants. She talks to other scientists. She talks to elders in different tribes.

Meet Donna House. She says you can learn a lot by taking walks outdoors with your elders.

Think Like a Scientist

Everyone can do science. To think like a scientist you have to:

- ask a lot of questions.

- find answers by investigating.

- try things over and over again.

- tell what really happens, not what you wanted to happen.

Do goldfish have eyelids? It looks like goldfish never close their eyes.

I read that goldfish do not have eyelids.

If the sunlight is too bright for their eyes, they swim to a shady spot.

Use Critical Thinking

Scientists use observations and other facts to answer their questions. A fact can be checked to make sure it is true. An opinion is what you think about the facts.

When you think, "That can't be true," you are thinking critically. Critical thinkers question what they hear.

Science Inquiry

You can use **science inquiry** to learn about the world around you. Say you are playing with magnets.

Observe It seems like when I hold the magnets one way, they push apart. When I turn one magnet, they stick.

Ask a Question I wonder, are some parts of round magnets stronger than other parts?

Form an Idea I think some parts of round magnets are stronger than others.

Experiment I will need a round magnet and some paper clips. I will count how many paper clips the round magnet picks up. I will test different places on the magnet. I will do each test a few times.

STANDARDS
4.a. Draw pictures that portray some features of the thing being described.
4.b. Record observations and data with pictures, numbers, or written statements.

4.e. Make new observations when discrepancies exist between two descriptions of the same object or phenomenon.

Conclusion I found that a round magnet picks up more paper clips on one side. So, my idea is supported. Round magnets do have parts that are stronger.

Communicate what you learn. You can use pictures, numbers, or words.

Inquiry Process

Here is how some scientists answer questions and make new discoveries.

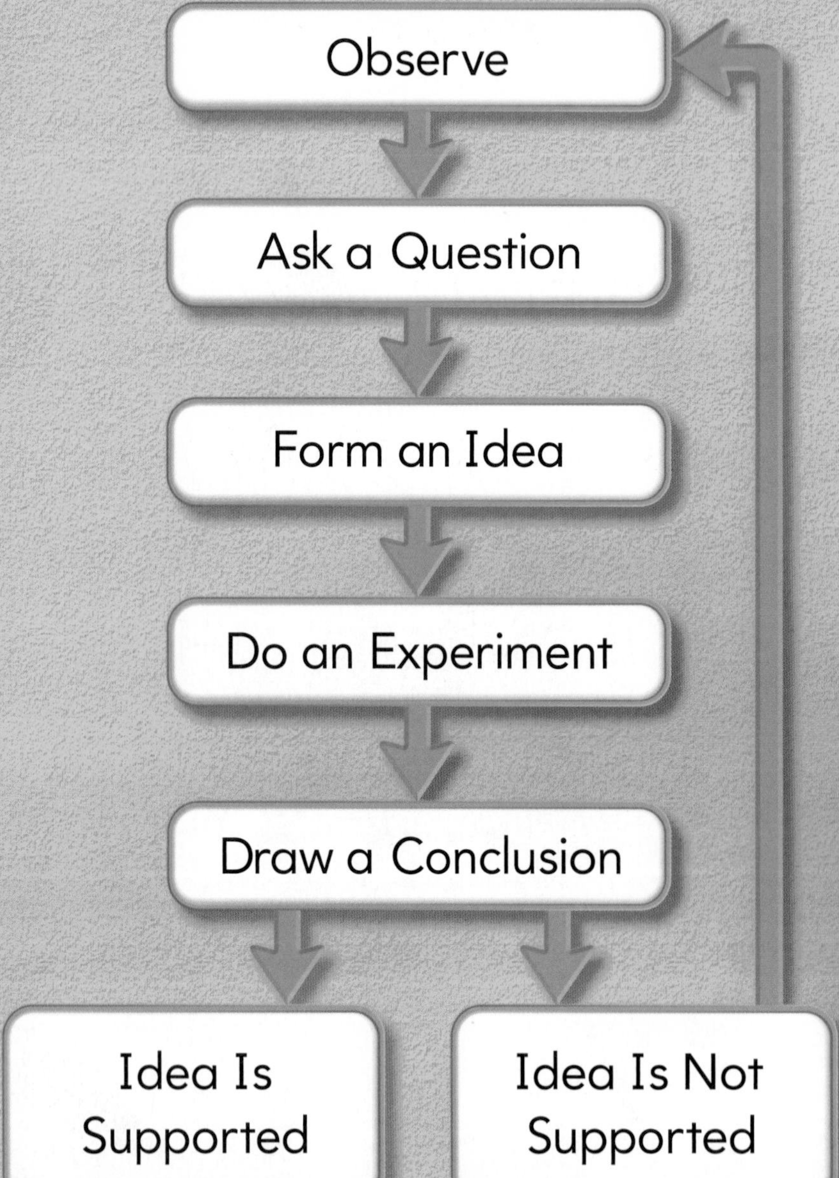

Observe

↓

Ask a Question

↓

Form an Idea

↓

Do an Experiment

↓

Draw a Conclusion

Idea Is Supported

Idea Is Not Supported

Try it Yourself!

Experiment With a Diving Squid

Squeeze the bottle. The squid sinks.
Stop squeezing. The squid floats.

1 What questions do you have about the squid?

2 How would you find the answers?

3 Make a plan to test your idea.
Tell what you think you will find out.

Be an Inventor

Neil Dermody had trouble finding his seat belt when he was eight years old. His mom asked him to invent a way to solve the problem.

First, Neil thought of putting light bulbs on the seat belt. He decided that the bulbs might break. Then he thought of things that glow in the dark.

Neil painted the buckle with paint that glowed in the dark. He sewed glow-in-the-dark fabric to the strap. It worked just fine.

Neil Dermody wins first prize for his invention.

"My mom always said, 'What problem are you having? How can you fix it?'"

What Is Technology?

The tools people make and use are **technology**. Paint that glows in the dark is technology. So is a hybrid car.

Scientists use technology. They use telescopes to study things that are far from Earth. They also use tools to measure things.

Technology can make life easier. Sometimes it causes problems too. Cars make it easy for people to travel. But a car's gas and oil can pollute the air.

A Better Idea

"I wish I had a better way to _____."
How would you fill in the blank?
Everyone can invent new things
and ideas. Even you!

An electric toothbrush
is fun to use. It also
cleans teeth better.

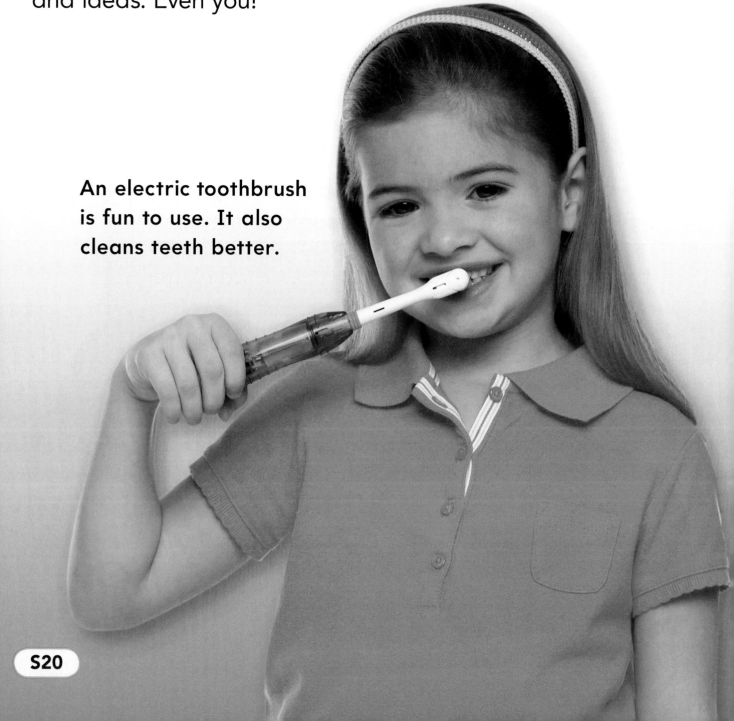

How to Be an Inventor

1. **Find a problem.** It may be at school, at home, or in your neighborhood.

2. **Think of a way to solve the problem.** List some ways to solve the problem. Decide which one will work best.

3. **Make a sample and try it out.** Your idea may need many materials or none at all. Try it out many times.

4. **Make your invention better.** Use what you learned to make changes.

5. **Share your invention.** Tell how your invention makes an activity easier or more fun. If it did not work well, tell why.

Make Decisions

Throwing Paper Away

How much paper does your class throw away? Most paper and other trash is buried in the ground. It takes up a lot of space.

Paper is made from mashed wood. Many trees are cut down to make paper. A lot of water is used. A lot of energy is used too.

Scrap Paper to Reuse

Deciding What to Do

How could your class throw away less paper?

Here's how to make your decision. You can use the same steps to help solve problems in your home or neighborhood.

Learn → Learn about the problem. Find the facts. You could talk to an expert or read a book.

List → List actions you could take. Add actions other people could take.

Decide → Decide which action is best for you, your school, or your neighborhood.

Share → Tell others what you decide.

Science Safety

Know the safety rules of your classroom and follow them. Follow the safety tips in your science book.

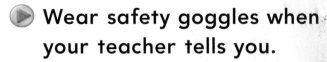 Wear safety goggles when your teacher tells you.

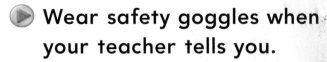 Keep your work area clean. Tell your teacher about spills right away.

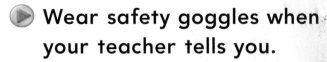 Learn how to care for the plants and animals in your classroom.

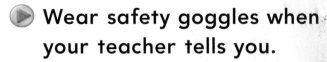 Wash your hands when you are done.

LIFE  SCIENCE

UNIT
A

Needs of Living Things

California Field Trip

Sea World

Killer whales, such as Shamu, are the largest members of the dolphin family.

Blood starfish find their food near sea sponges.

Adelie penguins can dive 500 feet underwater for food.

Needs of Living Things

California valley quails

California Big Idea!

Standard Set 2.
Life Sciences

Plants and animals meet their needs in different ways.

A Dragonfly

by Eleanor Farjeon

When the heat of the summer
Made drowsy the land,
A dragonfly came
And sat on my hand.

With its blue-jointed body,
And wings like spun glass,
It lit on my fingers
As though they were grass.

Chapter 1

Plants

Giant sequoias in
Yosemite National Park

LESSON 1

Strawberries are plants. What do plants need to grow?

LESSON 2

Buttercups have flowers and leaves. What are other plant parts?

LESSON 3

A plant's roots are below the ground. What do roots do?

LESSON 4

Leaves grow toward light. Why does this happen?

My Journal

Write or draw in your journal to answer the questions above.

Vocabulary

Picture Glossary

Vocabulary Skill

Break It Apart

sunlight

Find the two smaller words in this word. Say each word. Then say the words together.

leaves

Leaves are parts of a plant that make food for the plant.

roots

Roots are the parts of a plant that take in water from the ground.

soil

Soil is the loose top layer of Earth.

sunlight
Sunlight is light from the Sun.

Start with Your Standards

Standard Set 2. Life Sciences

2.a. *Students know* different plants and animals inhabit different kinds of environments and have external features that help them thrive in different kinds of places.

2.b. *Students know* both plants and animals need water, animals need food, and plants need light.

2.e. *Students know* roots are associated with the intake of water and soil nutrients and green leaves are associated with making food from sunlight.

Standard Set 4. Investigation and Experimentation covered in this chapter: 4.a., 4.b., 4.c., 4.e.

What Are the Needs of Plants?

Building Background

Plants need water, light, air, and space to grow.

Inquiry Skill

Measure Use a tool to find how much or how many.

 STANDARDS

2.b. *Students know* both plants and animals need water, animals need food, and plants need light.
4.c. Record observations on a bar graph.

What You Need

goggles

ruler

plant and water

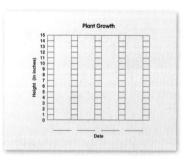

bar graph

Observe a Plant

Steps

STEP 1

1. **Measure** Use a ruler to measure a plant.
Safety: Wear goggles!

2. **Record Data** Record the height on a bar graph.

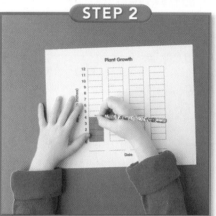
STEP 2

3. Keep the plant in a sunny place. Water the plant when needed.
Safety: Clean up spills!

4. **Measure** Each week, measure the plant again. Record the height.

STEP 3

Think and Share

1. **Compare** How did your graph compare with your classmates' graphs?

2. **Infer** What do plants need?

Guided Inquiry

Experiment Use what you know to **predict** how often you need to water a plant. Make a plan to check your prediction.

Vocabulary

sunlight

Reading Skill

Compare and Contrast

Compare	Contrast

STANDARDS

2.b. *Students know* both plants and animals need water, animals need food, and plants need light.

Needs of Plants

Plants need water, light, air, and space to live. Most plants get light from the Sun. Light from the Sun is called **sunlight**.

Some plants need a lot of light. Other plants do not need much light.

A healthy plant gets enough light, water, air, and space.

Which plant is not getting enough water?

Some plants need more water than other plants. A plant's leaves may sag if they do not get enough water. You can grow healthy plants if you know what they need.

Compare and Contrast How are the needs of plants alike?

Express Lab

Activity Card 1
Design a Garden

11

Space to Grow

Plants need space to get the air, sunlight, and water they need. Large plants need a lot of space to grow. Small plants do not need as much space as large plants.

Big trees need more space than small flowers.

Plants that do not have enough space may not grow very big. After you plant a garden, you may need to take out some plants. That will give the other plants more space.

Plants need space to grow.

 **Compare and Contrast** How are the needs of large plants and small plants different?

Lesson Wrap-Up

❶ **Vocabulary** What is **sunlight**?

❷ **Reading Skill** What are some ways that the needs of plants are different?

❸ **Measure** How can measuring a plant tell you if it is getting what it needs?

Technology Visit **www.eduplace.com/cascp** to find out more about the needs of plants.

STANDARDS 1–3: 2.b.

Plants and Machines

Many people grow plants for food. Farmers use machines to give plants what they need to grow.

Some places in California do not get enough rain. Then farmers use machines to water the plants.

Machines water plants.

STANDARDS

2.b. *Students know* both plants and animals need water, animals need food, and plants need light.

READING **LINK**

Sometimes people grow plants indoors. They use lights because the plants do not get enough sunlight to grow.

Lights help plants grow.

Sharing Ideas

1. **Write About It** How do farmers use machines to give plants what they need to grow?

2. **Talk About It** What are some different tools for watering plants?

What Are the Parts of Plants?

Building Background

Plants have different parts that help them get what they need to live.

Inquiry Skill

Compare Look for ways that objects are alike and different.

 STANDARDS

2.a. *Students know* different plants and animals inhabit different kinds of environments and have external features that help them thrive in different kinds of places.
4.a. Draw pictures that portray some features of the thing being described.

What You Need

goggles and paper towels

hand lens

2 plants

paper and crayons

Compare Plant Parts

Steps

1 Take both plants out of their pots. Carefully shake the dirt from the roots. **Safety:** Wear goggles!

STEP 1

2 **Observe** Use a hand lens. Look closely at the parts of each plant.

STEP 2

3 **Record Data** Draw pictures to show the parts of each plant.

4 Put the plants back in the pots. **Safety:** Wash your hands!

STEP 3

Think and Share

1. **Compare** What parts do both plants have?

2. **Compare** How are the plants different?

Guided Inquiry

Ask Questions Find a gardener who can answer your questions about different plant parts. **Communicate** what you find.

17

Plant Parts

Plants have parts. Most plants have roots, stems, and leaves. Some plants have flowers. Each part helps the plant in a different way.

Express Lab

Activity Card 2
Be a Plant Expert

Parts of Plants

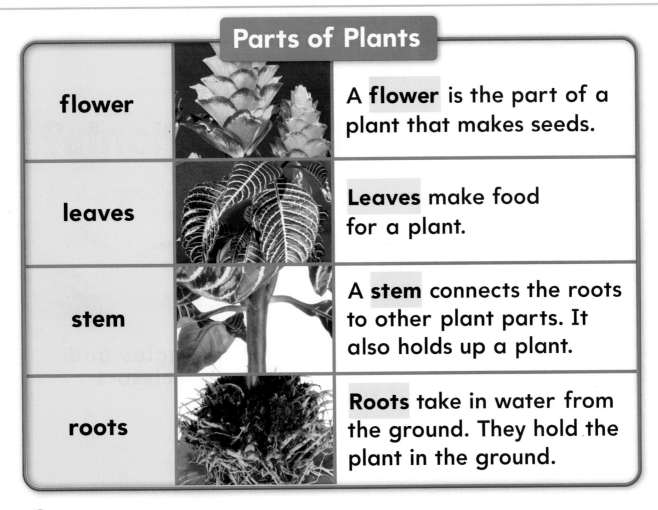

flower		A **flower** is the part of a plant that makes seeds.
leaves		**Leaves** make food for a plant.
stem		A **stem** connects the roots to other plant parts. It also holds up a plant.
roots		**Roots** take in water from the ground. They hold the plant in the ground.

Classify Which part of the plant makes food?

Lesson Wrap-Up

❶ **Vocabulary** What are the parts of a plant?

❷ **Reading Skill** Which part of a plant holds the plant in the ground?

❸ **Compare** How are plants alike?

Technology Visit **www.eduplace.com/cascp** to find out more about plant parts.

 STANDARDS 1: 2.a., 2: 2.e., 3. 2.a.

19

How Do Roots Help Plants?

Building Background

A plant's roots take in water and nutrients from the soil.

Inquiry Skill

Infer Use what you observe and know to tell what you think.

 STANDARDS

2.e. *Students know* roots are associated with the intake of water and soil nutrients and green leaves are associated with making food from sunlight.
4.b. Record observations and data with pictures, numbers, or written statements.

goggles and scissors

2 plants

labels

water

What Roots Do

Steps

1 **Experiment** Cut the roots off one plant. **Safety:** Wear goggles. Scissors are sharp!

2 Put the stem back in soil. Label the plant **no roots. Safety:** Wash your hands!

3 Label the other plant **roots.** Put the plants in a sunny place. Water them. Observe them for a week.

4 **Record Data** Write about how each plant changed.

STEP 1

STEP 2

STEP 3

Think and Share

1. How did each plant change?

2. **Infer** What do roots do for a plant?

Guided Inquiry

Experiment Cut the leaves off a new plant. **Predict** what will happen after one week. Check your prediction.

Learn by Reading

▶ **Vocabulary**

soil

nutrients

◎ **Reading Skill**

Main Idea and Details

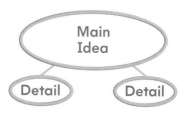

STANDARDS

2.e. *Students know* roots are associated with the intake of water and soil nutrients and green leaves are associated with making food from sunlight.

How Roots Work

The roots of most plants grow in soil. **Soil** is the loose top layer of Earth. **Nutrients** are materials in soil that plants need to grow. A plant's roots take in water and nutrients from the soil.

Water and nutrients move from the roots to other plant parts.

soil with plants

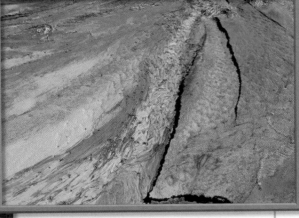

soil without plants

Roots help hold up a plant.
They also help keep the soil
in place. Soil can wash away
when there are no plants.

Main Idea How do roots
help a plant?

Express Lab

Activity Card 3
Observe Roots

23

Different Kinds of Roots

Different plants have different kinds of roots. A dandelion has a long main root. Grass has many small roots. A tree has large roots that hold it in the ground.

This plant has many small roots.

These roots take in nutrients near the top of the soil.

Some plants have roots that people and animals eat. Carrots and radishes are roots.

🎯 **Main Idea** What are some ways that roots look different?

People eat beet roots.

roots

Lesson Wrap-Up

❶ **Vocabulary** How does a plant get **nutrients**?

❷ **Reading Skill** What are two different kinds of roots?

❸ **Infer** What could happen to a plant if its roots were not in soil?

💻 **Technology** Visit **www.eduplace.com/cascp** to find out more about plants.

STANDARDS 1–3: 2.e.

How Do Leaves Help Plants?

Building Background

Leaves take in sunlight to make food for a plant. The plant gets energy from food.

Inquiry Skill

Experiment Make a plan, choosing the items to use and the steps to follow.

 STANDARDS

2.e. *Students know* roots are associated with the intake of water and soil nutrients and green leaves are associated with making food from sunlight.
4.e. Make new observations when discrepancies exist between two descriptions of the same object or phenomenon.

What You Need

2 plants

water

box

paper and crayons

Sunlight and Leaves

Steps

1. Water both plants. Put them in a sunny place.

2. **Experiment** Draw a picture of each plant. Cover one plant with a box.

3. **Compare** Look at the plants after one week. Draw how each plant looks now.

STEP 1

STEP 2

STEP 3

Think and Share

1. **Infer** Compare your drawings with those of others. What differences do you find?

2. **Experiment** If your drawings are different, try the experiment again. Did the results change?

Guided Inquiry

Experiment What will happen to the covered plant if you leave the cover off? **Predict** and then try it.

Vocabulary

energy

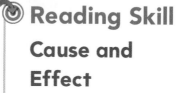

Reading Skill

Cause and Effect

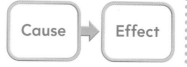

Cause → Effect

STANDARDS

2.e. *Students know* roots are associated with the intake of water and soil nutrients and green leaves are associated with making food from sunlight.
2.b. *Students know* both plants and animals need water, animals need food, and plants need light.

Energy from Sunlight

Plants need energy to live and grow. **Energy** is the power to cause change.

Plants get the energy they need from sunlight. Plants use sunlight, air, and water to make their own food.

Which plant is not getting enough light?

All plants need light. Plants will not grow well if they do not get the light they need. Leaves that do not get enough light may turn yellow or brown.

◎ **Cause and Effect** What happens if a plant does not get enough light?

How Leaves Work

Most plants have leaves. The leaves take in sunlight and air to make food for the plant.

The food moves from the leaves to other parts of the plant. The plant uses energy from the food to grow.

Sunlight

Different Kinds of Leaves

Leaves come in many shapes and sizes. Many leaves are flat. Some leaves have sharp points. Some trees have long, thin leaves called needles.

Pine trees have needles.

Holly leaves have sharp points.

 **Cause and Effect** What do leaves do for a plant?

oak leaf

Lesson Wrap-Up

❶ **Vocabulary** Where do plants get **energy**?

❷ **Reading Skill** What might cause a plant's leaves to turn yellow or brown?

❸ **Experiment** How can doing an experiment again help you check a prediction?

Technology Visit **www.eduplace.com/cascp** to find out more about plants.

STANDARDS 1–2: 2.e., 2.b., 3: 4.e.

STANDARDS **2.e.** *Students know* roots are associated with the intake of water and soil nutrients and green leaves are associated with making food from sunlight.

Super Leaf

This leaf is so big you can sit in it like a boat! The Victoria water lily has the largest leaves of any plant on Earth. Some Victoria lily pads grow to more than two meters across! That's wider than a grown–up is tall.

A two-meter lily pad could easily float a hundred frogs without sinking!

Victoria water lilies need lots of sunlight and very warm weather to grow so big.

My Journal

Find the biggest leaf you can. Calculate how many of your leaves add up to the width of a 2-meter water lily.

Math Find a Pattern

Look at the pattern of the leaves.

1. What is the pattern?

2. What color is likely to come next?

Writing Describe a Plant

What parts do plants have? Write sentences that tell about plant parts. Draw a picture of your plant.

Ernesto Sandoval

Earth is home to many different plants. Collecting and growing plants is the job of Ernesto Sandoval. He works at a greenhouse in Davis, California. Mr. Sandoval makes sure plants get the air, water, light, and nutrients they need.

Visual Summary

Plants need sunlight, water, air, and space. They have parts that help them meet their needs.

| Plants need air, water, light, and space to live. | Plants have parts that help them get what they need. | Roots take in water and nutrients from soil. | Leaves take in sunlight and air to make food. |

My Journal

Review your answers to the Lesson Preview questions.

STANDARDS 2.a., 2.b., 2.e.

Main Ideas

1. What does a plant need to live? (p. 10)

2. How do roots help a plant? (pp. 22–23)

3. How do leaves help plants? (p. 30)

Vocabulary

Choose the correct word from the box.

4. The power to cause change

5. The part of a plant that connects the roots to other plant parts

6. The loose top layer of Earth

7. Materials in the soil that help plants grow

energy (p. 28)
nutrients (p. 22)
soil (p. 22)
stem (p. 19)

Using Science Skills

8. You and a friend get different results when you do a plant experiment. How can you find out who is right?

9. **Critical Thinking** How can people help plants that do not get what they need?

STANDARDS 1: 2.b., 2–3: 2.e., 4: 2.b., 2.e., 5: 2.a., 6–7: 2.e., 8: 4.e., 9: 2.b.

Chapter 2

Animals

Black bear

LESSON 1

Animals need air, food, and water. How do animals get what they need?

LESSON 2

Jackrabbits have strong back legs. How do you think they use them?

LESSON 3

A horse eats plants. What kind of teeth does a horse have?

My Journal

Write or draw in your journal to answer the questions above.

39

Vocabulary Preview

Vocabulary

Picture Glossary
English-Spanish p. H18

Vocabulary Skill

Use What's After

fins

wings

The ending **-s** has been added to these words. The ending means "more than one." Tell what each word means.

fins
Fins are body parts that fish use to move.

wings
Wings are body parts that birds use to fly.

meat eater

A meat eater is an animal that has sharp teeth to tear food.

shelter

A shelter is a safe place for animals to live.

Start with Your Standards

Standard Set 2. Life Sciences

2.a. *Students know* different plants and animals inhabit different kinds of environments and have external features that help them thrive in different kinds of places.

2.b. *Students know* both plants and animals need water, animals need food, and plants need light.

2.c. *Students know* animals eat plants or other animals for food and may also use plants or even other animals for shelter and nesting.

2.d. *Students know* how to infer what animals eat from the shape of their teeth (e.g., sharp teeth: eats meat; flat teeth: eats plants).

Standards Set 4. Investigation and Experimentation covered in this chapter: 4.b., 4.d.

What Are the Needs of Animals?

Building Background

Animals need food, air, and water to live. They find those things where they live.

Inquiry Skill

Work Together Share what you observe with a partner.

What You Need

hermit crab in its home

hermit crab food

water

 STANDARDS

2.b. *Students know* both plants and animals need water, animals need food, and plants need light.
4.d. Describe the relative position of objects by using two references (e.g., above and next to, below and left of).

An Animal's Needs

Steps

① Put the hermit crab home in a safe place. Give the hermit crab water and food.

STEP 1

② **Work Together** Watch what the hermit crab does. Use words such as **above** and **next to** to tell where it goes.

STEP 2

③ **Record Data** Draw pictures. Show how the hermit crab gets what it needs to live.

STEP 3

Think and Share

1. **Work Together** Talk with your partner. How does a hermit crab use its home?

2. **Infer** What do animals need to live?

Guided Inquiry

Ask Questions Finish this question. How much food and water does a _____ need? **Work together** to find the answers.

► **Vocabulary**

shelter

◎ **Reading Skill**

Draw Conclusions

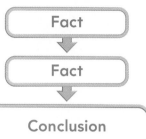

Fact

↓

Fact

↓

Conclusion

STANDARDS

2.b. *Students know* both plants and animals need water, animals need food, and plants need light.
2.c. *Students know* animals eat plants or other animals for food and may also use plants or even other animals for shelter and nesting.

Animals Need Food

Animals need food, air, and water. Animals eat food when they are hungry. Plants and other animals are food for animals. Big animals need more food than small animals.

These cows are eating plants.

An eagle needs a larger shelter than a hummingbird.

Shelter

Some animals need a shelter. A **shelter** is a safe place for animals to live. Some animals find shelter in plants or other animals. Many animals build shelters such as nests. Some animals, such as whales, do not use shelters at all.

Draw Conclusions
How are the needs of big and small animals alike?

Express Lab

Activity Card 5
Investigate Shelters

Animals Need Air and Water

All animals need air and water to live. Animals have body parts to help them get air. Many animals use their nose to breathe in air. Fish need air, too. They have gills to take in air from water.

gill

A tiger has a nose for breathing.

Whales come to the top of water to get air.

How is this mule deer getting what it needs?

Most animals get water by drinking. Some animals get water from the food they eat.

Draw Conclusions What would happen if an animal did not get air and water?

Lesson Wrap-Up

❶ **Vocabulary** How does an animal use a **shelter**?

❷ **Reading Skill** How are all animals alike?

❸ **Work Together** How can sharing ideas help you learn more about animals?

Technology Visit **www.eduplace.com/cascp** to find out more about the needs of animals.

 STANDARDS 1: 2.c., 2–3: 2.b.

Animal Needs

How do different animals meet their needs? Five animal friends are about to find out!

Cast

Robin
Deer
Frog
Fish
Turtle

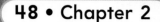

STANDARDS

2.b. *Students know* both plants and animals need water, animals need food, and plants need light.

READING LINK

Deer: Hello, Robin. Hello, Frog. What are you doing here?

Frog: I am looking for food. I like to catch insects with my long tongue.

Robin: I'm here to find food for my babies. They like to eat worms.

Deer: I drink water from the lake. I eat leaves off bushes and trees.

Robin: I built my nest with twigs from bushes. My babies are safe in the nest now.

Frog: Oh dear! I'm not safe! I see a hawk in the sky. I have to go.

Deer: Frog, why don't you hide under the water? Frog?

Turtle: Frog has hopped away. But I can answer your question.

Deer: Please do!

Turtle: Frog cannot breathe under water. So he finds shelter behind a rock.

Fish: I can breathe under water. I can find shelter in the water, too.

Turtle: I take my shelter with me! I can tuck my head and legs into my shell.

Deer: Wow! We're lucky. We all can find everything we need right here where we live!

Sharing Ideas

1. **Write About It** Choose an animal. Write about how it meets its needs.
2. **Talk About It** Give hints about how an animal meets its needs. Have classmates guess the animal.

What Are the Parts of Animals?

Building Background

Body parts help animals get what they need to live.

Inquiry Skill

Classify Group living things that are alike in some way.

What You Need

animal pictures

crayons and paper

STANDARDS

2.a. *Students know* different plants and animals inhabit different kinds of environments and have external features that help them thrive in different kinds of places.
4.b. Record observations and data with pictures, numbers, or written statements.

Animal Parts

Steps

1. **Compare** Look at the pictures. Tell how the animals are alike and different.

2. **Classify** Sort the animal pictures into groups that are alike in one way.

3. **Record Data** Name your groups. Draw pictures or write names to show the animals in each group.

STEP 1

STEP 2

STEP 3

Think and Share

1. **Classify** How did you group the animals?

2. **Infer** How might an animal use its long neck?

Guided Inquiry

Ask Questions Think of questions about how animals use body parts. Make a plan to find answers. **Communicate** what you find.

Vocabulary

fins

wings

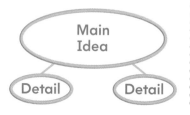

Reading Skill

Main Idea and Details

Main Idea

Detail   Detail

STANDARDS

2.a. *Students know* different plants and animals inhabit different kinds of environments and have external features that help them thrive in different kinds of places.

Animal Body Parts

Animals use their body parts to find food and to stay safe. Animals use their eyes, ears, noses, legs, tails, and other parts to help them live.

Bush Baby

Large eyes help it see at night.

Ears help it find insects to eat.

Gray fur helps it hide in trees.

Legs and fingers help it catch food and hold on to trees.

Using Body Parts to Stay Safe

quills

stinger

claws

smell

sound

color and shape

Some animals can use body parts to hurt other animals or scare them away. Some animals have colors or shapes that help them hide.

Main Idea What body parts help animals find food?

Express Lab

Activity Card 6
Model Feathers

Parts for Moving

Animals have body parts that they use to move. Animals move to find food. They move to get away from enemies.

A fish uses its tail and **fins** to move in water. A lion uses its strong legs to run and climb.

tail

fin

leg

wing

A bird uses its **wings** to fly through the air. A bird also uses its legs to walk, hop, and hold on to trees.

 **Main Idea** How does a bird use its legs?

Lesson Wrap-Up

❶ Vocabulary How does a fish use **fins** to live in water?

❷ Reading Skill Why do many animals have legs?

❸ Classify What kinds of body parts help animals stay safe?

Technology Visit **www.eduplace.com/cascp** to find out more about animal body parts.

 STANDARDS 1–3: 2.a.

How Do Animals Use Their Mouths?

Building Background

Some animals have sharp teeth. Others have flat teeth. You can tell what an animal eats by looking at its teeth.

Inquiry Skill

Use Models Use something like a real thing to learn how the real thing works.

What You Need

human teeth model

pictures of animal teeth

paper and crayons

STANDARDS

2.d. *Students know* how to infer what animals eat from the shape of their teeth (e.g., sharp teeth: eats meat; flat teeth: eats plants).
4.b. Record observations and data with pictures, numbers, or written statements.

Sharp or Flat

Steps

STEP 1

1 **Use Models** Observe the shapes of the model teeth.

2 Think about the kinds of food you eat. Record how you use your different teeth.

STEP 2

3 **Compare** Look at the animal pictures. Decide which human teeth are like the teeth of each animal.

STEP 3

Think and Share

1. **Compare** What tooth shape would be helpful for tearing?

2. **Infer** How might the shape of an animal's teeth affect the kind of food it eats?

Guided Inquiry

Ask Questions Think about questions you have about the kinds of teeth different animals have. **Work together** to make a plan to find answers.

Reading Skill

Compare and Contrast

Compare	Contrast

STANDARDS

2.d. *Students know* how to infer what animals eat from the shape of their teeth (e.g., sharp teeth: eats meat; flat teeth: eats plants).

Flat Teeth or Sharp Teeth

You can group animals by what they eat. A **plant eater** eats mostly plants. That kind of animal has flat teeth. It uses its teeth to grind plants.

Zebras are plant eaters.

A lion is a meat eater.

A **meat eater** eats other animals. Meat eaters have sharp teeth. Their teeth help them tear meat.

Some animals have both flat teeth and sharp teeth. These animals eat both plants and animals.

Compare and Contrast How are a lion's teeth different from a zebra's teeth?

Express Lab

Activity Card 7
Observe Teeth

Other Mouth Parts

Not all animals have teeth. Some animals have different mouth parts to help them eat.

A housefly has a mouth part that takes in water like a sponge.

A chameleon uses its long tongue to catch food.

Birds have beaks. A long beak helps a bird drink from a flower. Sharp beaks help birds crack open seeds.

A pelican has a large beak for catching fish.

Compare and Contrast How is a pelican's mouth different from a chameleon's mouth?

Lesson Wrap-Up

❶ **Vocabulary** What kind of teeth does a **plant eater** have?

❷ **Reading Skill** How are a plant eater's teeth different from meat eater's teeth?

❸ **Use Models** How can a model of teeth help you understand what animals eat?

📖 **Technology** Visit **www.eduplace.com/cascp** to find out more about animal mouth parts.

 STANDARDS 1–3: 2.d.

Super Tongue

What *is* this bushy beast? It's not make-believe! It's the giant anteater of Central America and South America.

The giant anteater is as long as a door is tall. It looks odd, but its body parts are perfect for an anteater!

The anteater's tongue is as long as your arm. It is rough and sticky. That helps it trap ants.

▼ **Snout** Its snout is long, but its mouth is very small.

A giant anteater eats thousands of ants each day.

My Journal

How is an anteater's mouth right for the food it eats? Write your ideas in your journal.

Math Picture Graph

Look at the chart of children's pets that have four legs.

Mr. Williams's Class	
Pet with Four Legs	Number of Pets
cat	IIII
dog	III
hamster	I
turtle	II

Use the data to make a picture graph. Are there more cats or dogs?

Writing Describe a Place

Write about a place where an animal lives. Tell what the place looks like. Explain how the animal gets what it needs there.

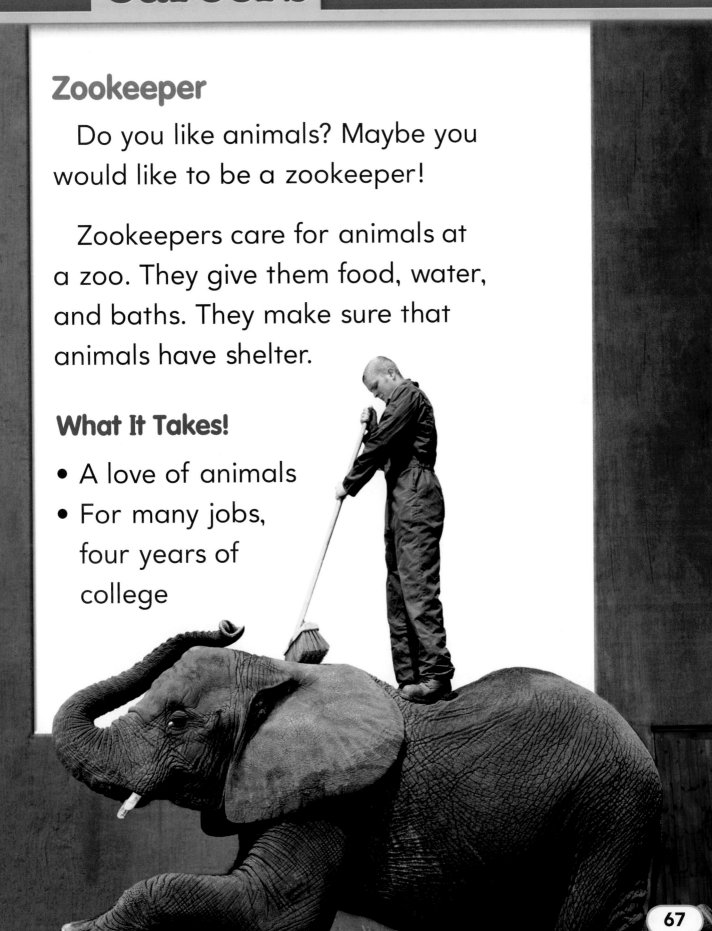

Zookeeper

Do you like animals? Maybe you would like to be a zookeeper!

Zookeepers care for animals at a zoo. They give them food, water, and baths. They make sure that animals have shelter.

What It Takes!

- A love of animals
- For many jobs, four years of college

Visual Summary

Animals have body parts that help them get what they need.

Animals need air, food, and water.

Animals have parts for moving, breathing, and staying safe.

Animals have different kinds of teeth for eating plants and meat.

My Journal

Review your answers to the Lesson Preview questions.

STANDARDS 2.a., 2.b., 2.c., 2.d.

Main Ideas

1. What do animals need to live? (p. 44)

2. How does a bush baby use its body parts? (p. 54)

3. Where do animals find shelter? (p. 45)

Vocabulary

Choose the correct word from the box.

4. Parts of a bird that it uses to fly through the air

5. A safe place for animals to live

6. Parts of a fish that help it move

7. An animal that eats mostly plants

fins (p. 56)

plant eater (p. 60)

shelter (p. 45)

wings (p. 57)

Using Science Skills

8. Draw a picture of a meat eater's teeth. Then draw a picture of a plant eater's teeth. Label the pictures.

9. **Critical Thinking** Why isn't a bicycle an animal?

STANDARDS 1: 2.b., 2: 2.a., 3: 2.c., 4: 2.a., 5: 2.c., 6: 2.a., 7: 2.d., 8: 2.d., 4.b., 9: 2.b.

69

Test Practice

Choose the correct answer.

1. Birds use their _____ to fly.

   fins   wings   legs
   ○   ○   ○

2. Plants and animals both need _____ to live.

   water   soil   shelter
   ○   ○   ○

3. A plant's leaves turn yellow if it does not get enough _____.

   soil   flowers   sunlight
   ○   ○   ○

4. Which picture shows an animal that only eats plants?

   ○   ○   ○

5. A plant's _____ take in water and nutrients from soil.

flowers   roots   stems
○   ○   ○

6. Many animals need _____ to stay safe.

shelter   food   water
○   ○   ○

Checking Main Ideas

Write the correct answer.

7. What can you infer about animals that have both flat teeth and sharp teeth?

8. What needs are being met for these baby birds?

STANDARDS 1: 2.a., 2: 2.b., 3: 2.e., 4: 2.d., 5: 2.e., 6: 2.c., 7: 2.d., 8: 2.b., 2.c.

You Can...

Discover More

What bird flaps its wings the fastest?

A hummingbird flaps its wings about 75 times every second! The wings move so fast that they make a humming sound. Hummingbirds are called nature's helicopters because of the way they move.

 Simulations Go to **www.eduplace.com/cascp** to learn more about the parts of a hummingbird.

Where Plants and Animals Live

California Connection

Visit www.eduplace.com/cascp to find out where some California plants and animals live.

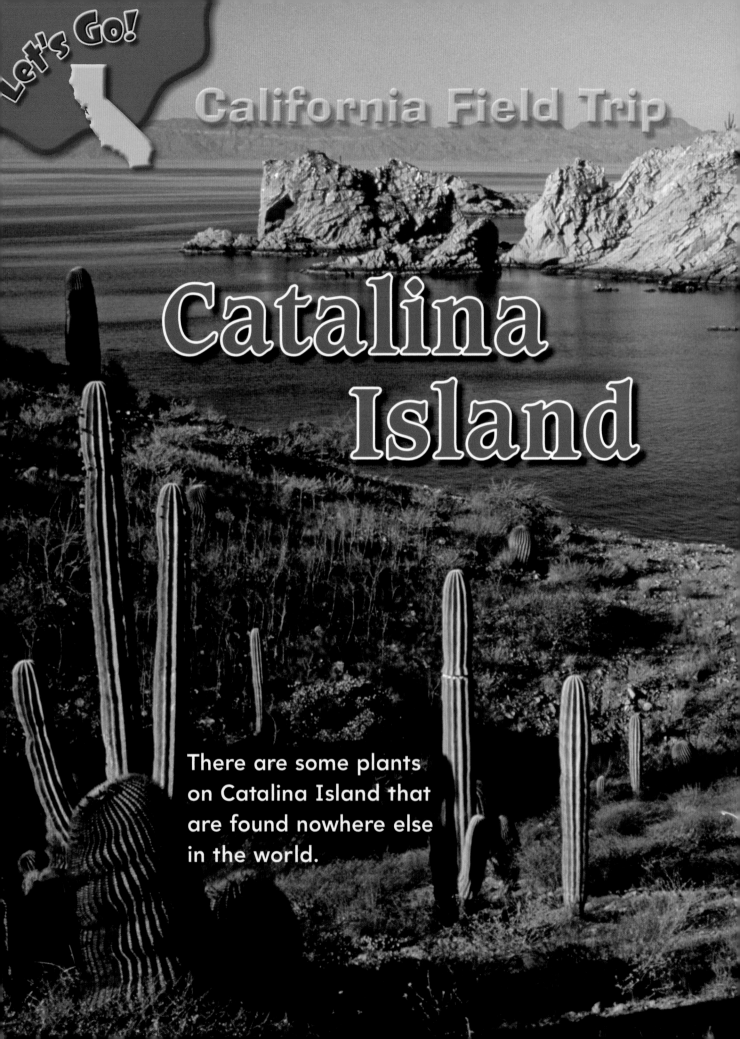

Let's Go!

California Field Trip

Catalina Island

There are some plants on Catalina Island that are found nowhere else in the world.

St. Catherine's lace is only found growing naturally on Catalina Island.

The Catalina Island rattlesnake has no rattle on its tail.

Where Plants and Animals Live

Loggerhead turtle

California **Big Idea!**

Standard Set 2.
Life Sciences

Plants and animals meet their needs in different ways.

Environments

The habitat of a plant or animal

Is the place where it can thrive,

Where it gets water, food, and
   shelter,

So it can grow and change and
   survive.

 from *Science Songs*, track 7

Chapter 3

Living Things Meet Their Needs

Dolphins off the coast of California

LESSON 1

An environment has living and nonliving things. What are some living things?

LESSON 2

Deer get energy from eating plants. What are other ways animals get energy?

LESSON 3

A fox finds shelter in a hollow log. Where else do animals find shelter?

LESSON 4

Some desert animals hide during the day. Why do they do that?

My Journal

Write or draw in your journal to answer the questions above.

Vocabulary

Picture Glossary
English-Spanish p. H18

Vocabulary Skill

Use Pictures

food chain

Look at the picture of a food chain. A picture helps you know the meaning of the words. What do you know about a food chain from this picture?

living thing
A living thing needs air, food, water, and space.

nonliving thing
A nonliving thing does not need air, food, and water.

food chain
A food chain shows how energy moves from one thing to another.

environment

An environment is all of the living and nonliving things around a living thing.

Start with Your Standards

Standard Set 2. Life Sciences

2.a. *Students know* different plants and animals inhabit different kinds of environments and have external features that help them thrive in different kinds of places.

2.b. *Students know* both plants and animals need water, animals need food, and plants need light.

2.c. *Students know* animals eat plants or other animals for food and may also use plants or even other animals for shelter and nesting.

Standard Set 4. Investigation and Experimentation covered in this chapter: 4.a., 4.b., 4.d.

What Is an Environment?

Building Background

An environment has living things and nonliving things. There are many different kinds of environments.

Inquiry Skill

Classify Group objects that are alike in some way.

What You Need

hand lens

drawing paper

crayons

STANDARDS

2.a. *Students know* different plants and animals inhabit different kinds of environments and have external features that help them thrive in different kinds of places.
4.d. Describe the relative position of objects by using two references (e.g. above and next to, below and left of).

Environments

Steps

1. **Observe** Find a small rock or a log. Look for living things and nonliving things. Use two words, such as **below** and **left**, to tell where you find things.

2. **Classify** Decide whether each thing you find is living or nonliving.

3. **Record Data** Make a chart. Draw the living and nonliving things you find.

STEP 1

STEP 2

STEP 3

Think and Share

1. Where did you see the most living things? Tell why.

2. **Compare** How are all of the living things alike?

Guided Inquiry

Experiment Look in a different place. Follow the same steps. **Compare** the two charts that you made.

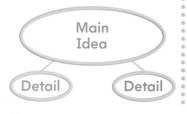
Environments

An **environment** is all the living and nonliving things around a living thing. A **living thing** needs air, food, water, and space. Plants and animals are living things.

A **nonliving thing** does not need food, water, and air. Water, rocks, and soil are nonliving things.

Alpine Tundra

What living things are in this environment?

Rain Forest

Ocean

▲ A rain forest is warm and wet. Many plants and animals get what they need there.

◀ Ocean animals find what they need in the water.

🎯 **Main Idea** What can you find in an environment?

Express Lab

Activity Card 8
Draw an Environment

Different Environments

There are many kinds of environments. Some are hot. Others are cold. Some environments are wet. Others are dry. Many environments are hot sometimes and cold at other times.

Prairie

A prairie is hot and dry in summer. It is cold in winter.

Desert

Many deserts are hot and dry most of the time.

Arctic

It is cold most of the year in an arctic environment.

Main Idea In what ways are environments different?

Lesson Wrap-Up

❶ **Vocabulary** What is an **environment**?

❷ **Reading Skill** What kinds of living things do you find in an environment?

❸ **Classify** Name three things that living things need.

Technology Visit **www.eduplace.com/cascp** to find out more about environments.

 STANDARDS 1–2: 2.a., 3: 2.b.

How Do Living Things Get Energy?

Building Background

Living things get energy they need from food. Animals eat plants or other animals for food.

Inquiry Skill

Use Models Use something like a real thing to learn how the real thing works.

What You Need

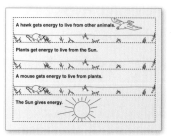

A hawk gets energy to live from other animals.

Plants get energy to live from the Sun.

A mouse gets energy to live from plants.

The Sun gives energy.

food-chain strips

scissors

glue

Food Chain

Steps

1. Cut out food-chain strips.
   Safety: Scissors are sharp!

2. Find the Sun strip. Glue the ends to make a loop.

3. **Use Models** Add loops in the order of the clues on the strips. There's your food chain!

4. **Communicate** Talk to a partner. Tell what a food chain is.

STEP 1

STEP 2

STEP 3

Think and Share

1. Why did your food chain model start with the Sun?

2. **Infer** Why does a hawk need plants to live?

Guided Inquiry

Ask Questions Ask what some other animals eat. Use the answers to make a new food chain. **Communicate** how the links connect.

◎ **Reading Skill**

Sequence

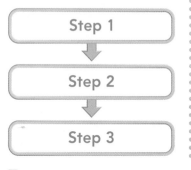

STANDARDS

2.c. *Students know* animals eat plants or other animals for food and may also use plants or even other animals for shelter and nesting.
2.b. *Students know* both plants and animals need water, animals need food, and plants need light.

Food and Energy

Energy is the power to cause change. Living things get the energy they need from food.

Plants use sunlight to make their own food. The food gives the plants energy to grow and change.

Young wasps get energy by eating part of a hornworm.

Mule deer eat only plants.

Spiders hunt
and eat insects.

Animals get energy from the food they eat. They eat plants or other animals. Their food gives them energy to grow and change.

Sequence How do animals get energy?

Express Lab

Activity Card 9
Write a Food Chain Song

Food Chains

A **food chain** shows the order in which energy moves from one thing to another. Almost all food chains start with the Sun. Energy can move from the Sun, to plants, to animals, and to people.

1 Seaweed uses sunlight to make food.

2 A small fish eats the seaweed.

3 A large fish eats the small fish.

1 Grass gets energy from the Sun.

2 A cow eats the grass.

3 A child drinks a cow's milk.

Sequence Tell the order in which energy moves from the Sun to the child.

Lesson Wrap-Up

① **Vocabulary** What is **energy**?

② **Reading Skill** In a food chain, what happens after the Sun helps plants grow?

③ **Use Models** What does a food chain show?

Technology Visit **www.eduplace.com/cascp** to find out more about food chains.

STANDARDS 1–3: 2.b., 2.c.

STANDARDS 2.a. *Students know* different plants and animals inhabit different kinds of environments and have external features that help them thrive in different kinds of places.

Plants That Hunt

Gotcha! A fly smells sweet sap. It crawls between two spiky leaves to eat some dinner. The leaves snap shut. Now the fly is the *plant's* dinner!

Most plants get enough food from soil and water. Venus flytraps live in places with poor soil. They catch and eat insects to get more food.

Sticky trap A sundew ▷
plant traps insects
with sticky hairs on its
leaves. Then the leaf
folds around the insect
and eats it!

◁ **Watch out! A California
pitcher plant is slippery
inside! Insects slide into
the plant and drown in
a pool of liquid.**

My Journal

If a plant lived in
good soil, do you think
the plant would have to
catch insects? Write your
ideas in your journal.

93

Where Do Animals Find Shelter?

Building Background

Animals find shelter in plants, on other animals, and under the ground. Some animals build shelters.

Inquiry Skill

Ask Questions When you ask questions about what you observe, you can learn more about your world.

What You Need

hand lens

drawing paper

crayons

 STANDARDS

2.c. *Students know* animals eat plants or other animals for food and may also use plants or even other animals for shelter and nesting.
4.a. Draw pictures that portray some features of the thing being described.

Animal Homes

Steps

STEP 1

1 **Observe** Walk around outside your school. Look for ways that animals use plants. Use a hand lens to see small places.

STEP 2

2 **Record Data** Draw pictures of the animal homes you find.

STEP 3

3 **Ask Questions** Make a list of questions about how animals use plants for homes. Work with a partner to find answers.

Think and Share

1. **Infer** What animals might live in the homes you found?

2. How do animals use plants?

Guided Inquiry

Experiment Try changing a plant's environment. **Work together** with a partner. Talk about what happens when environments change.

Vocabulary

shelter

Reading Skill
Classify

Group	Group

STANDARDS

2.c. *Students know* animals eat plants or other animals for food and may also use plants or even other animals for shelter and nesting.

Animals Find Shelter

Many animals need shelter. **Shelter** is a safe place for animals to live. Many animals find shelter in plants, in the ground, or in water.

A deer finds shelter under a tree.

Tiny fleas sometimes find shelter on a dog or cat.

flea

Some animals find shelter on other animals. A hermit crab lives in another animal's shell. Some animals live right on the skin of another animal.

A clownfish stays safe on an anemone.

⊙ **Classify** What animals live on other animals?

Express Lab

Activity Card 10
Observe Shelter

A beaver builds a lodge with sticks, mud, and grasses.

Animals Build Shelters

Many animals build their own shelters. They use things they find in their environment. Birds may use twigs, mud, and even feathers to build their nests.

This loon builds a nest near water.

Insects build homes in many places. Some insects, such as ants, live under the ground. Other insects, such as wasps, may build their nests in trees.

 **Classify** **Name three animals that build their own shelters.**

Wasps build paperlike nests from wood and saliva.

 **Lesson Wrap-Up**

❶ **Vocabulary** What is a **shelter**?

❷ **Reading Skill** Name three animals that use plants to build shelters.

❸ **Ask Questions** How can asking questions about animal shelters be helpful?

Technology Visit **www.eduplace.com/cascp** to find out more about animal shelters.

How Do Plants and Animals Live in Different Places?

Building Background

Living things have parts that help them live in different kinds of environments.

Inquiry Skill

Infer Use what you observe and know to tell what you think.

STANDARDS

2.a. *Students know* different plants and animals inhabit different kinds of environments and have external features that help them thrive in different kinds of places.
4.a. Draw pictures that portray some features of the thing being described.

What You Need

backgrounds

animal cutouts

crayons

glue stick

Hidden Animals

Steps

1 **Observe** Look at a background. Color an animal so that it looks like the background.

STEP 1

2 Glue your animal on the background to hide it.

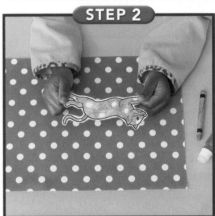
STEP 2

3 **Compare** Trade pictures with a classmate. Try to find the hidden animal.

Think and Share

1. Why was the paper animal able to hide on the colored background?

2. **Infer** Tell how you think an animal's body color helps it hide outside.

STEP 3

Guided Inquiry

Ask Questions Finish this question. How does a ___'s body shape help it hide? **Work together** to find an answer.

◎ **Reading Skill**

Draw Conclusions

Fact

↓

Fact

↓

Conclusion

STANDARDS

2.a. *Students know* different plants and animals inhabit different kinds of environments and have external features that help them thrive in different kinds of places.

Parts Help Living Things

Plants and animals live in different environments. They each have **structures**, or parts, that help them live in their environments.

A big beak helps a macaw crack nuts. ▶

A kangaroo rat has long feet for hopping on sand and rocks.

The living things on these two pages have structures that help them get what they need.

Draw Conclusions Why are living things able to live in different environments?

A giraffe's long neck helps it reach food high in trees. ▶

▲ Long stems on water lilies let the leaves reach sunlight.

Express Lab

Activity Card 11
Act Out an Animal

Structures That Protect

Plants and animals have structures that protect them in their environment. Many animals have body coverings that help them hide. Some plants have parts that keep animals from eating them.

A rose has thorns that keep animals from eating it.

Why is it hard to see this fish? ▼

Draw Conclusions How do structures help an animal?

A camel has wide feet that help it walk in sand. ▶

◀ Hooves help mountain goats climb on rocks.

Lesson Wrap-Up

❶ **Vocabulary** What are **structures** of living things?

❷ **Reading Skill** How is a camel able to live in a sandy desert environment?

❸ **Infer** Why is a polar bear's white fur helpful?

Technology Visit **www.eduplace.com/cascp** to find out more about structures of living things.

Read to find out about the snowshoe hare in winter and in summer.

In a Winter Meadow

by Jack Prelutsky

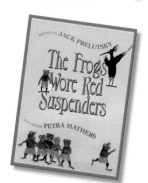

In a winter meadow
icy breezes blow,
snowshoe hares are running
softly through the snow.

Up and down they scurry,
darting left and right,
snowshoe hares are running,
dressed in winter white.

STANDARDS

2.a. *Students know* different plants and animals inhabit different kinds of environments and have external features that help them thrive in different kinds of places.

READING **LINK**

Animal Disguises

by Belinda Weber

Snowshoe hares live in Alaska. In the summer their coats are brown in order to blend in with the ground. In the winter the hares grow new, white coats to help them stay hidden in the snow.

Sharing Ideas

1. **Write About It** How are snowshoe hares protected in winter?

2. **Talk About It** Why is brown a good color for a snowshoe hare in summer?

107

LINKS
for Home and School

Math Make a Counting Book

Make a counting book. On the first page, draw one living thing. Write the number 1 on the page. Make seven more pages. Add one living thing each time.

1. How many living things are on your last page?

2. How many more things are on the third page than are on the first page?

Writing Write a Story

Write a story about a plant or an animal in its environment. Be sure to include the parts that help the plant or animal live in that place.

Dr. Jennifer Caselle

Meet Dr. Jennifer Caselle. She is a biologist. She studies fish that live along the coast of California. She knows that some fish are in trouble! People are catching too many of them.

To help the fish, Dr. Caselle makes safe places for fish to live. These places are called reserves. Fishing is not allowed in the reserves.

Dr. Caselle is collecting fish so that she can count them.

Visual Summary

Living things need air, food, water, and space. They each have structures that help them get what they need.

| An environment has what the plants and animals that live there need. |
| Living things get energy from food. |
| Many animals use plants or other animals for shelter. |
| Living things have structures that help them live in their environments. |

Review your answers to the Lesson Preview questions.

STANDARD 2.a., 2.b., 2.c.

Main Ideas

1. How do some animals use plants for shelter? (pp. 98–99)

2. How do plants use sunlight? (p. 88)

3. How do body coverings keep animals safe? (p. 104)

Vocabulary

Choose the correct word from the box.

4. Parts

5. All the living and nonliving things around a living thing

6. A safe place for animals to live

7. The order in which energy moves from one thing to another

environment
(p. 82)
food chain
(p. 90)
shelter (p. 96)
structures
(p. 102)

Using Science Skills

8. Draw a picture of plants and animals in an environment.

9. **Critical Thinking** Why do animals need both living things and nonliving things?

STANDARDS 1: 2.c., 2: 2.b., 3–5: 2.a., 6: 2.c., 7: 2.b., 2.c., 8: 4.a., 9: 2.b.

111

Chapter 4

Kinds of Environments

Elephants in Africa

LESSON 1

Mew gulls live along a coast. What other animals live along a coast?

LESSON 2

Mallards live in streams and lakes. How do they find what they need there?

LESSON 3

Pikas live high in the mountains. What body parts help them live there?

My Journal

Write or draw in your journal to answer the questions above.

Vocabulary Preview

Vocabulary

habitat p. 118

coast p. 118

stream p. 126

mountain p. 134

Picture Glossary

English-Spanish p. H18

Vocabulary Skill

Use Words

coast

Sometimes words have more than one meaning. See how a word is used in a sentence to tell which meaning to use.

habitat
A habitat is the part of an environment where a plant or animal lives.

coast
A coast is a land and water habitat along an ocean.

mountain
A mountain is a high part of Earth's surface.

stream

A stream is a small river.

Start with Your Standards

Standard Set 2. Life Sciences

2.a. *Students know* different plants and animals inhabit different kinds of environments and have external features that help them thrive in different kinds of places.

Standard Set 4. Investigation and Experimentation covered in this chapter: 4.b.

What Lives Along a Coast?

Building Background

A coast can be cold and rocky. Plants and animals have parts to help them live there.

Inquiry Skill

Predict Use what you know to tell what you think will happen.

 STANDARDS

2.a. *Students know* different plants and animals inhabit different kinds of environments and have external features that help them thrive in different kinds of places.
4.b. Record observations and data with pictures, numbers, or written statements.

What You Need

paper towel

fiberfill

ice cubes in a bag

Keeping Warm

Steps

① Put a paper towel on your arm. Put a bag of ice on the paper towel. Record how your arm feels.

STEP 1

② **Predict** Will fiberfill help keep your skin warm? Write down what you think.

STEP 2

③ **Record Data** Put fiberfill between the paper towel and the bag of ice. Record how your arm feels.

STEP 3

Think and Share

1. Did the fiberfill help keep your skin warm? Why do you think that happened?

2. **Infer** How does a thick body covering help an animal that lives along a coast?

Guided Inquiry

Experiment Do the same activity. Use other materials between the paper towel and the ice bag. **Observe** what happens.

Vocabulary

habitat

coast

Reading Skill

Main Idea and Details

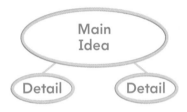

STANDARDS

2.a. *Students know* different plants and animals inhabit different kinds of environments and have external features that help them thrive in different kinds of places.

A wandering tattler eats fish and other small animals.

A Coast Habitat

A part of an environment where a plant or an animal lives is its **habitat**. A **coast** is a land and water habitat along an ocean.

Many living and nonliving things are found in a coast habitat. A coast habitat has air, salty water, sand, rocks, plants, and animals.

Plants live in the sand and rocks along a coast. Animals live on the land and in the water. They eat plants and animals that live there.

A periwinkle is a sea snail. It eats tiny plantlike food.

Main Idea Why is a coast a good place for a sea lion?

Sea lions find food in the water. They rest on rocks.

Express Lab

Activity Card 12
Make a Coast Habitat

Life Along a Coast

Some living things have parts to help them live along a coast. Strong roots and stems help plants grow in sand and rocks.

Animals along a coast have parts that help them find food. They also have parts that keep them warm in cold ocean water.

Channel Islands

Pelicans have large mouths to hold fish. They have webbed feet for swimming.

Whales swim along a coast. They have fat, called blubber, that keeps them warm.

Main Idea What parts help a pelican live along the coast?

Lesson Wrap-Up

❶ Vocabulary What is the land and water habitat along an ocean called?

❷ Reading Skill What are some parts that help plants and animals live on a coast?

❸ Predict How can you predict where an animal might live?

Technology Visit **www.eduplace.com/cascp** to find out more about coast habitats.

 STANDARDS 1–3: 2.a.

STANDARDS 2.a. *Students know* different plants and animals inhabit different kinds of environments and have external features that help them thrive in different kinds of places.

Blushing Giants

Have you ever seen a *pink* walrus? Turning pink is how a walrus cools off when it gets hot.

A walrus has thick fat called blubber. Blubber keeps it warm in the cold ocean. But blubber can make the walrus too hot in sunlight. So the walrus' body sends blood to its skin to cool it off. This turns the walrus pink.

Hippos turn pink, too! When they get hot, they sweat a pink slime that protects them from the Sun.

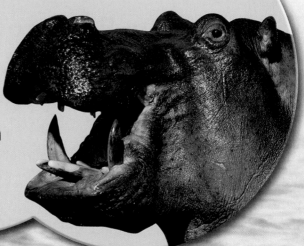

A walrus does not use its big teeth to eat. It uses them to pull itself onto slippery ice.

My Journal

What might happen if a walrus went to live in a warm place? Write your ideas in your journal.

What Lives in a Stream?

Building Background

Plants and animals have structures to help them live in wet places.

Inquiry Skill

Use Models Use something like a real thing to learn how the real thing works.

 STANDARDS

2.a. *Students know* different plants and animals inhabit different kinds of environments and have external features that help them thrive in different kinds of places.
4.b. Record observations and data with pictures, numbers, or written statements.

What You Need

large pan

clay

rocks and pebbles

water

Make a Stream

Steps

1. **Use Models** Use clay to make a stream in a pan. Then make the banks of the stream with more clay.

STEP 1

2. Put rocks and pebbles in the bottom of the stream.

STEP 2

3. **Observe** Pour water in one end of the stream. Watch the water flow.

4. Write about what happened.

STEP 3

Think and Share

1. **Communicate** Tell a classmate about the nonliving parts of the stream.

2. **Infer** How might living things meet their needs in a stream habitat?

Guided Inquiry

Experiment Plan ways to change how the water moves in your model. **Observe** what happens each time.

Reading Skill

Draw Conclusions

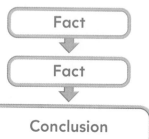

Fact

↓

Fact

↓

Conclusion

STANDARDS

2.a. *Students know* different plants and animals inhabit different kinds of environments and have external features that help them thrive in different kinds of places.

A Stream Habitat

A **stream** is a small river. Many living and nonliving things are found in a stream habitat. A stream habitat has animals and plants. It has air, fresh water, rocks, and soil.

Water in a stream helps plants that grow nearby.

Living things find what they need in a stream habitat. Animals drink water. They eat plants and animals in or near the stream.

Raccoons find food in a stream.

Draw Conclusions What nonliving things in a stream do animals use?

Rocks make hiding places for small animals.

Express Lab

Activity Card 13
Jump Like a Frog

127

Life in a Stream

Living things have parts that help them live in a stream habitat. Some plants have long stems that let the leaves reach sunlight. A heron uses long legs to walk in water.

Draw Conclusions How does a turtle's shell help it in a stream habitat?

turtle

bass

minnow

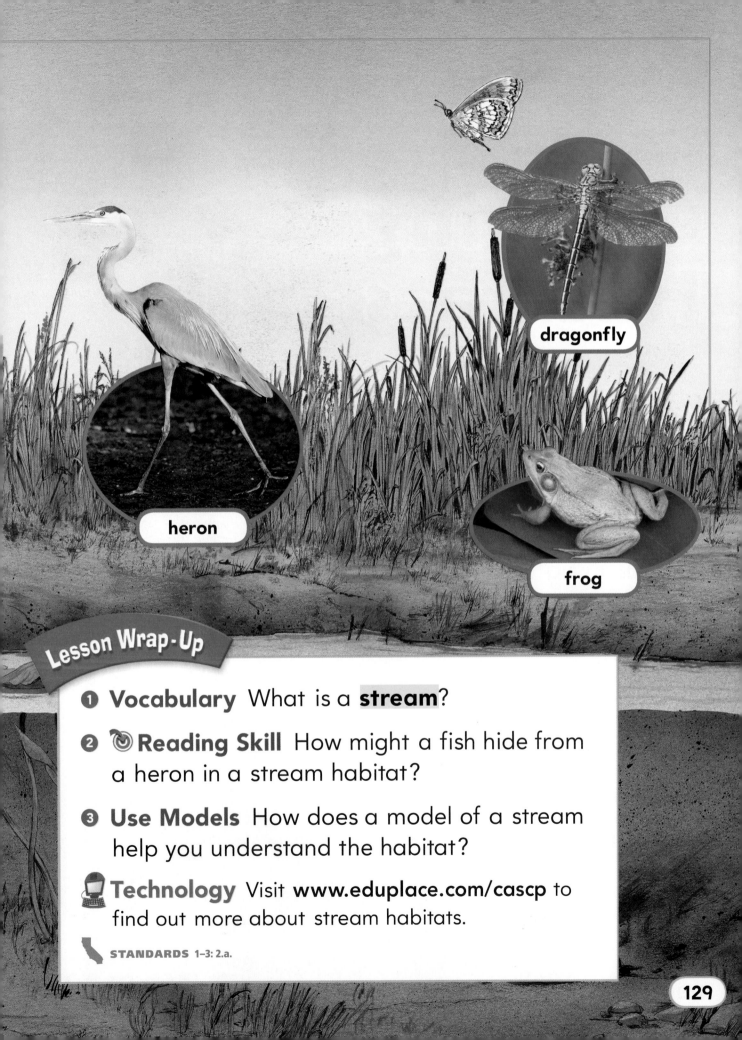

dragonfly

heron

frog

Lesson Wrap-Up

① Vocabulary What is a **stream**?

② Reading Skill How might a fish hide from a heron in a stream habitat?

③ Use Models How does a model of a stream help you understand the habitat?

Technology Visit **www.eduplace.com/cascp** to find out more about stream habitats.

STANDARDS 1–3: 2.a.

Creating Habitats

Aquariums and zoos have habitats made by people. The San Diego Zoo has a habitat called Monkey Trails and Forest Tales. This small habitat is like a habitat in nature.

Machines were used to move trees to make the forest habitat.

STANDARDS

2.a. *Students know* plants and animals inhabit different kinds of environments and have external features that help them thrive in different kinds of places.

READING **LINK**

The Monkey Trails and Forest Tales habitat has more than 30 kinds of African and Asian animals. People can observe monkeys from a walkway in the trees.

Sharing Ideas

1. **Write About It** How can visiting the San Diego Zoo help people learn about science?

2. **Talk About It** Why do you think zoo workers spend time studying habitats?

131

What Lives on a Mountain?

Building Background

Mountaintops can be cold and windy. Plants and animals have parts that help them live there.

Inquiry Skill

Observe Use your senses to learn about things around you.

What You Need

picture cards

Mountain Life	
Sentences	**Plant or Animal**
1. Hooves help animals walk on mountain rocks.	
2. Wind and snow can change the shapes of mountain plants.	
3. Thick fur helps keep animals warm in cold weather.	
4. In a mountain forest, plants near the ground get little light.	

mountain life chart

 STANDARDS

2.a. *Students know* different plants and animals inhabit different kinds of environments and have external features that help them thrive in different kinds of places.
4.b. Record observations and data with pictures, numbers, or written statements.

Mountain Life

Steps

STEP 1

1. **Observe** Look at the first sentence on the chart. Then look at the pictures. Find a picture that matches the sentence.

STEP 2

2. **Communicate** Tell a partner why you think the picture matches the sentence.

3. **Record Data** Write the name of the plant or animal next to the sentence.

STEP 3

4. Match the rest of the sentences with pictures.

Think and Share

1. How do parts help plants and animals live on a mountain?

2. **Compare** How are the living things alike?

Guided Inquiry

Ask Questions What questions can you ask to find out more about mountain plants and animals? **Compare** your questions with a partner.

A Mountain Habitat

A **mountain** is a high part of Earth's surface. Different plants and animals live on different parts of a mountain.

Many plants and animals live on the lower part of a mountain. Only a few things live on a mountaintop.

mountain bluebird

The lower part of a mountain has warmer weather than the top. There are many trees and plants. It is easy for animals to find food and shelter.

🎯 **Compare and Contrast** How is the top of a mountain different from the lower part of a mountain?

California dogface

Yosemite National Park

Express Lab

Activity Card 14
Make a Model of a Mountain

Living on Mountaintops

Mountaintops can be cold and windy. They have few trees. Mountaintops have a lot of rocks. They have little soil or water. Plants and animals have parts that help them live on mountaintops.

Marmots have thick fur to keep them warm.

Bighorn sheep have hooves like rubber. The hooves help the sheep walk on steep rocks.

Plants grow close to the ground. Wind cannot blow them away.

◎ Compare and Contrast

Why are there more animals and plants at lower levels of a mountain?

Lesson Wrap-Up

❶ Vocabulary What is a **mountain**?

❷ ◎ Reading Skill How are living things different on high and low parts of a mountain?

❸ Observe How can you use your senses to learn about mountain life?

Technology Visit www.eduplace.com/cascp to find out more about mountain habitats.

STANDARDS 1–3: 2.a.

Math Number Sentences

Use counters to find the answers.
Then write the number sentences.

1. How many seals in all are along the coast?

2. If two seals dive into the water, how many seals will be left?

Writing Describe a Place

Draw a stream picture. Include plants and animals in your picture. Write about the stream you drew.

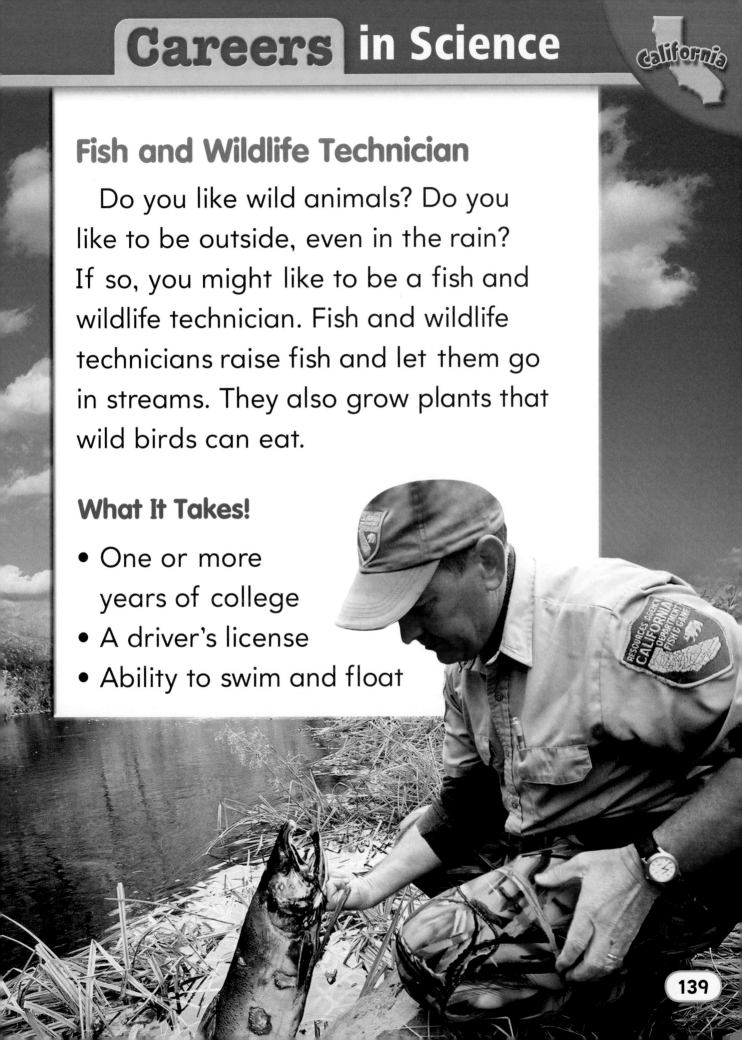

Fish and Wildlife Technician

Do you like wild animals? Do you like to be outside, even in the rain? If so, you might like to be a fish and wildlife technician. Fish and wildlife technicians raise fish and let them go in streams. They also grow plants that wild birds can eat.

What It Takes!

- One or more years of college
- A driver's license
- Ability to swim and float

Visual Summary

Different plants and animals live in different environments. They have parts to help them meet their needs.

Environments

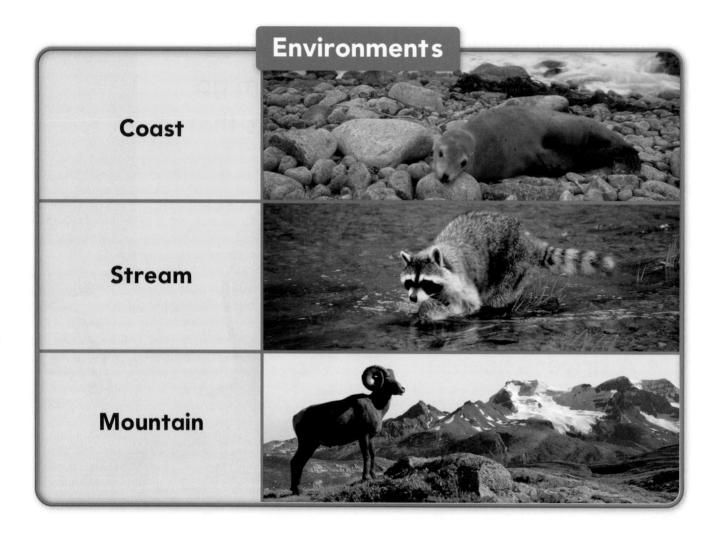

Coast	
Stream	
Mountain	

Review your answers to the Lesson Preview questions.

STANDARDS 2.a.

Main Ideas

1. Where do sea lions and pelicans live? (pp. 119–120)

2. Why do many plants grow in a stream habitat? (pp. 126–127)

3. Why are there few living things on mountaintops? (p. 136)

Vocabulary

Choose the correct word from the box.

4. A small river

5. A high part of Earth's surface

6. A habitat along an ocean

7. Part of an environment where plants and animals live

coast (p. 118)
habitat (p. 118)
mountain (p. 134)
stream (p. 126)

Using Science Skills

8. Observe living things in an environment. Write about how they meet their needs.

9. **Critical Thinking** A toad needs fresh water. Where might it live? Explain.

Test Practice

Choose the correct answer.

1. Living things need air, water, and _____.

   food   trees   mountains
   O   O   O

2. Plants and animals need _____ to grow.

   shelter   leaves   energy
   O   O   O

3. Which of these things do plants need to make food?

   O   O   O

4. What is a safe place for animals to live?

   shelter   store   food chain
   O   O   O

5. Some animals use other _____ for shelter.

animals ○

light ○

food chains ○

6. Which structure helps a giraffe reach food high in trees?

spotted skin ○

long tail ○

long neck ○

Checking Main Ideas

Write the correct answer.

7. How do some animals use a stream to meet their needs?

8. Explain how this food chain works.

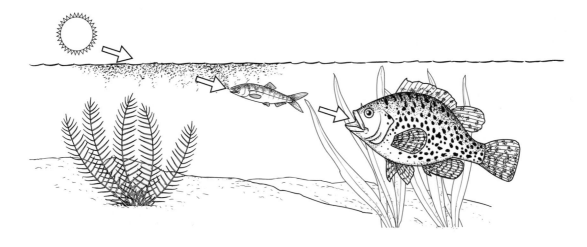

You Can...

Discover More

Why do you find shells on the beach?

Some ocean animals are covered with a hard shell. The hard shell protects the animal's soft body. After the animal dies, the shell is empty. Waves push the empty shell onto the beach.

 Simulations Go to **www.eduplace.com/cascp** to visit the underwater world of shells.

EARTH

UNIT C

SCIENCE

Weather Patterns

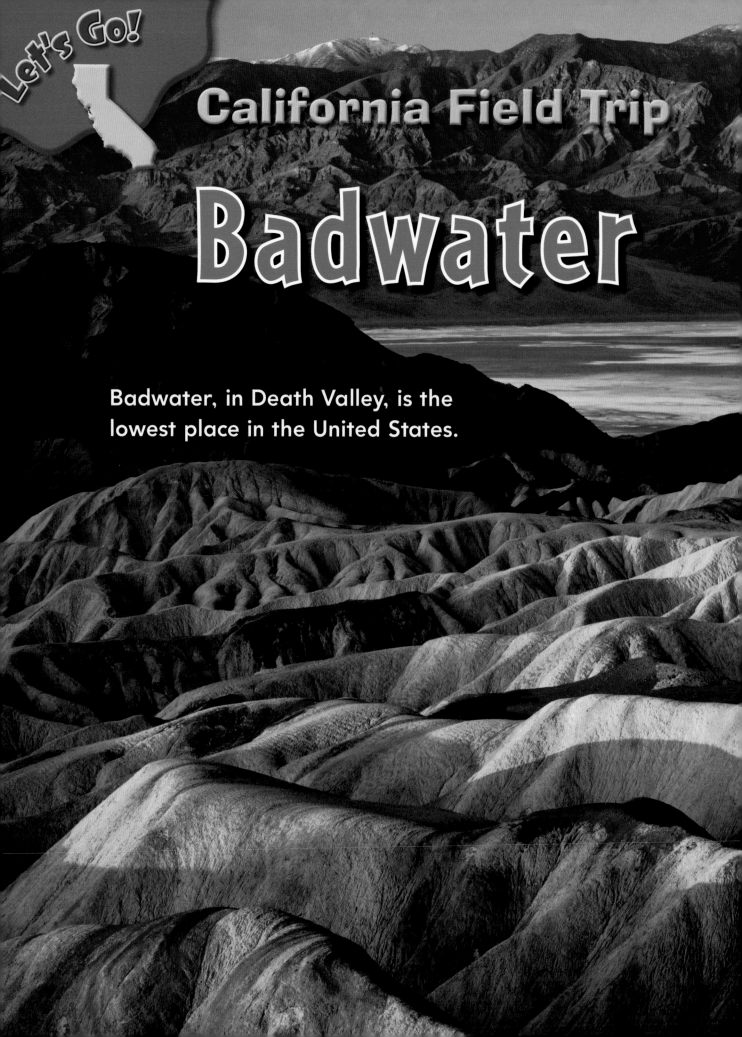

Let's Go!

California Field Trip

Badwater

Badwater, in Death Valley, is the lowest place in the United States.

Scorpion weed only grows in California, New Mexico, and Nevada.

Salt mixes with rainwater to form these interesting salt beds.

Weather Patterns

Rainbow over San Francisco Bay

California Big Idea!

Standard Set 3.
Earth Sciences

Weather can be observed, measured, and described.

City Rain

by Rachel Field

Rain in the city!
  I love to see it fall
Slantwise where the buildings crowd
  Red brick and all.
Streets of shiny wetness
  Where the taxis go,
With people and umbrellas all
  Bobbing to and fro.

Chapter 5

Weather

Golden Gate Bridge in
San Francisco, California

LESSON 1

Weather changes from day to day. How is today's weather different from yesterday's weather?

LESSON 2

You can use tools to find out about weather. What does a thermometer tell you?

LESSON 3

The Sun's energy warms things. What are some things that the Sun warms?

My Journal

Write or draw in your journal to answer the questions above.

Vocabulary Preview

Vocabulary

weather p. 154

thermometer p. 162

temperature p. 162

wind vane p. 164

energy p. 170

shadow p. 172

Picture Glossary
English-Spanish p. H18

Vocabulary Skill

Use Words

thermometer

You can use a thermometer to find out how hot the air is. Find other words in the sentence to help you know what a thermometer is.

thermometer
A thermometer is a tool that measures temperature.

wind vane
A wind vane shows which way the wind is blowing.

shadow
A shadow forms when an object blocks light.

weather
Weather is what the air outside is like.

Start with Your Standards

Standard Set 3. Earth Sciences

3.a. *Students know* how to use simple tools (e.g., thermometer, wind vane) to measure weather conditions and record changes from day to day and across the seasons.

3.b. *Students know* that the weather changes from day to day but that trends in temperature or rain (or snow) tend to be predictable during a season.

3.c. *Students know* the sun warms the land, air, and water.

Standards Set 4. Investigation and Experimentation covered in this chapter: 4.b., 4.e.

How Does Weather Change?

Building Background

When you record weather data, you see how weather changes from day to day.

Inquiry Skill

Record Data You can show what you observe with pictures, numbers, or words.

 STANDARDS

3.b. *Students know* that the weather changes from day to day but that trends in temperature or rain (or snow) tend to be predictable during a season.
4.b. Record observations and data with pictures, numbers, or written statements.

What You Need

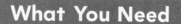

weather chart

weather pictures

scissors

glue

Record Weather

Steps

① **Observe** Look outside to see the weather today.

STEP 1

② Cut out pictures that show the weather today.
Safety: Scissors are sharp!

STEP 2

③ **Record Data** Glue the pictures in your weather chart.

④ Repeat steps 1 through 3 each day for one week.

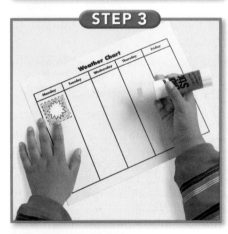
STEP 3

Think and Share

1. What does your chart tell you about weather?

2. Why might you record two pictures for the same day?

Guided Inquiry

Experiment Record weather data for two more weeks. **Compare** the data from week to week. Explain what you find.

◎ **Reading Skill**

Main Idea and Details

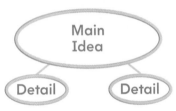

Main Idea

Detail Detail

◤ **STANDARDS**

3.b. *Students know* that the weather changes from day to day but that trends in temperature or rain (or snow) tend to be predictable during a season.

Kinds of Weather

Weather is what the air outside is like. There are many kinds of weather. Weather may be warm or cool. It may be rainy or sunny. It may be cloudy. It may be windy.

▲ **windy and cloudy**

◀ **rainy**

How do you know that it is warm and sunny here?

You can use your senses to observe the weather. You can see clouds. You can hear rain. You can feel warm or cool air. You can see wind move things.

Main Idea What are some kinds of weather?

Express Lab

Activity Card 15
Draw the Weather

Ways Weather Changes

Monday	cloudy	
Tuesday	rainy	
Wednesday	sunny	

Weather Changes

Weather can change from day to day. One day the weather can be sunny and warm. The next day it can be cloudy and cool. Then clouds may bring rain.

Cumulus clouds can turn gray and bring rain.

 **Main Idea** How might weather change from day to day?

Lesson Wrap-Up

❶ **Vocabulary** Tell something that you know about **weather**.

❷ 🎯 **Reading Skill** How can you use your senses to observe weather?

❸ **Record Data** Tell one way to record data.

⌨ **Technology** Visit **www.eduplace.com/cascp** to find out more about weather.

STANDARDS 1–2: 3.b., 3: 4.b.

STANDARDS 3.b. *Students know* that the weather changes from day to day but that trends in temperature of rain (or snow) tend to be predictable during a season.

Take Cover!

Flash, crash, rumble! Lightning creates the thunder that gives thunderstorms their special name.

The giant spark of electricity in this picture lights up a dangerous partner. It is called a tornado. A tornado is a very strong wind that twists in a circle as it moves. Tornadoes have the fastest winds on Earth!

▲ Only the strongest, most powerful thunderstorms, like this, produce damaging tornadoes.

My Journal

Talk to a weather expert. Find out how to stay safe when there are tornadoes or lightning. Write what you find.

How Are Weather Tools Used?

Building Background

Weather tools help people see how weather changes from day to day.

Inquiry Skill

Measure Use a tool to find how much or how many.

 STANDARDS

3.a. *Students know* how to use simple tools (e.g., thermometer, wind vane) to measure weather conditions and record changes from day to day and across the seasons.
4.b. Record observations and data with pictures, numbers, or written statements.

What You Need

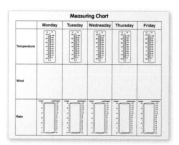

measuring chart

windsock

thermometer

rain collector and ruler

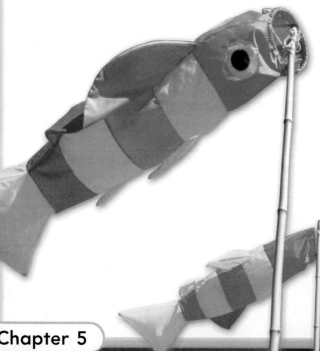

Use Weather Tools

Steps

STEP 1

1. Take a thermometer, a rain collector, and a windsock outside.

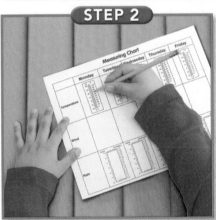

STEP 2

2. **Record Data** Read the thermometer. Record the temperature. Observe the windsock. Draw what you see.

STEP 3

3. **Measure** Use a ruler to measure any rain. Record what you measure. Empty the rain collector.

4. Do these steps for five days.

Think and Share

1. How do tools help you learn about weather?

2. **Predict** Look at your chart. Predict the temperature for tomorrow.

Guided Inquiry

Ask Questions Write questions about weather at other times of the year. Find answers by using weather tools to **measure**.

Vocabulary

thermometer
temperature
wind vane

Reading Skill
Draw
Conclusions

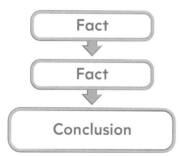

Fact

Fact

Conclusion

STANDARD

3.a. *Students know* how to use simple tools
(e.g. thermometer, wind vane) to measure
weather conditions and record changes from
day to day and across the seasons.

A Tool for Temperature

One way to tell about
weather is to use tools. A
thermometer is a tool that
measures temperature.
Temperature is how warm
or cool something is.

**What do these
thermometers tell
about weather?**

When the temperature is cold, you wear clothes that keep you warm. When it is hot, you wear clothes that help you cool off.

 **Draw Conclusions** If you need a coat, what can you tell about the temperature?

Express Lab

Activity Card 16
Master Measuring Rainfall

Tools for Wind and Rain

You can use tools to measure wind and rain. A windsock and a **wind vane** are tools that show which way the wind blows. A rain gauge measures rainfall.

Draw Conclusions If a rain gauge is full, what can you tell about the weather?

windsock

wind vane

rain gauge

① **Vocabulary** What is a **thermometer**?

② **Reading Skill** If a windsock is hanging down, what can you tell about the weather?

③ **Measure** How can you describe the weather?

Technology Visit **www.eduplace.com/cascp** to find out more about weather tools.

STANDARDS 1–2: 3.a., 3: 4.b.

Temperature Tools

Tools to measure temperature have been around for a long time.

Thermoscope Galileo Galilei built a thermoscope with a glass tube and water.

> The lowest floating tag tells the temperature.

Thermometer Daniel Gabriel Fahrenheit invented a thermometer.

> Liquid moves up the tube when it gets warm.

STANDARD

3.a. *Students know* how to use simple tools (e.g., thermometer, wind vane) to measure weather conditions and record changes from day to day and across the seasons.

READING LINK

Today, there are many different kinds of thermometers. Some thermometers have numbers next to a tube of liquid. Other thermometers only show numbers.

The world's largest thermometer is in Baker, California.

Sharing Ideas

1. **Write About It** Do you think a thermometer or a thermoscope is easier to use? Why?

2. **Talk About It** What happens inside Galileo's thermoscope when the temperature changes?

What Warms Land, Air, and Water?

Building Background

Earth gets energy from the Sun. The Sun warms Earth's land, air, and water.

Inquiry Skill

Use Data When two people get different results, you should check again.

 STANDARDS

3.c. *Students know* the sun warms the land, air, and water.
4.e. Make new observations when discrepancies exist between two descriptions of the same object or phenomenon.

What You Need

3 jars

water and sand

3 thermometers

heat chart

The Sun's Warmth

Steps

1. Fill one jar with water. Fill another jar with sand. Leave one jar empty.

2. **Measure** Put a thermometer in each jar. Read each thermometer. Record the temperature.

3. **Record Data** Put the jars in a sunny place. Record the temperatures every 30 minutes.

STEP 1

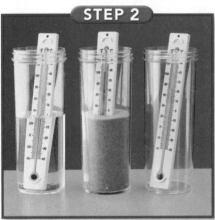

STEP 2

STEP 3

Think and Share

1. **Use Data** How did the temperature of each jar change?

2. **Infer** What do your results tell you about how the Sun changes temperature?

Guided Inquiry

Experiment Are your data the same as the data of others? If not, check your results. **Use data** you collect to decide why results were different.

▶ **Vocabulary**

energy
shadow

◎ **Reading Skill**
Cause and Effect

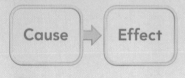

STANDARD

3.c. *Students know* the sun warms the land, air, and water.

Warmth from the Sun

Energy from the Sun warms Earth's land, air, and water. **Energy** is the power to cause change.

The Sun warms sand and sidewalks. It warms lakes and ponds. It warms you when you are in sunlight.

Big Sur is warmed by the Sun.

Air, land, and water feel warmer during the day. That is because the Sun is shining on them. The Sun does not warm things at night.

Cause and Effect Why is it cooler at night than during the day?

Express Lab

Activity Card 17
Compare Temperatures

Shadows

A **shadow** forms when an object blocks light. The place where a shadow forms is called shade. You feel cooler when you move from a sunny place to a shady place.

Where are the shadows?

Clouds make shadows on the land.

Clouds can block sunlight. That is why air may feel cooler on cloudy days. Clouds may bring rain.

Cause and Effect Why might it be cooler when it is raining?

Lesson Wrap-Up

❶ **Vocabulary** What does **energy** from the Sun do?

❷ **Reading Skill** What causes a shadow?

❸ **Use Data** How can you check your data if you and a classmate have different results?

 **Technology** Visit **www.eduplace.com/cascp** to find out more about the Sun's warmth.

STANDARDS 1–2: 3.c., 3: 4.e.

173

Math Compare Temperatures

Monday

Tuesday

Wednesday

Thursday

Compare. Write <, =, or > for each blank.

1. The temperature on Monday was _____ than the temperature on Wednesday.

2. The temperature on Tuesday was _____ than the temperature on Monday.

3. The temperature on Thursday was _____ than the temperature on Wednesday.

Writing Describe a Person

Talk to someone you know. Find out what kind of weather that person likes. Then write about the person.

Meteorologist

Meteorologists study the weather. They explain today's weather. They predict the weather for tomorrow. That helps people be ready when storms come.

What It Takes!

- A college degree in science
- An interest in weather and people

Visual Summary

Weather is what the air outside is like. You can use tools to tell about weather.

Weather

Weather changes from day to day.	**Monday** 	**Tuesday**	**Wednesday**

You can use weather tools.	

The Sun warms land, air, and water.	

My Journal

Review your answers to the Lesson Preview questions.

STANDARDS 3.a., 3.b., 3.c.

Main Ideas

1. What are some ways weather changes? (pp. 156–157)

2. What is a tool that shows which way the wind is blowing? (p. 164)

3. What are some things the Sun can warm? (p. 170)

Vocabulary

Choose the correct word from the box.

energy (p. 170)
shadow (p. 172)
temperature (p. 162)
thermometer (p. 162)

4. A tool that measures temperature

5. How warm or cool something is

6. The power to cause change

7. What forms when light is blocked

Using Science Skills

8. How can measuring and recording data with numbers help you understand weather?

9. **Critical Thinking** How do you know that it is windy if you cannot see the wind?

STANDARDS 1: 3.b., 2: 3.a., 3: 3.c., 4–5: 3.a., 6–7: 3.c., 8: 4.b., 9: 3.b.

Chapter 6

Seasons

Trees in fall

LESSON 1

People wear warmer clothes in winter. Why do they do that?

LESSON 2

Many plants bloom in spring. Why does that happen?

LESSON 3

People go to beaches more often in summer. Why do they do that?

LESSON 4

Aspen leaves change color in fall. How does weather change in fall?

My Journal

Write or draw in your journal to answer the questions above.

Vocabulary

Picture Glossary
English-Spanish p. H18

Vocabulary Skill

Classify Words

season

A **season** is a time of year. Say the names of all the seasons.

winter
Winter is the season that follows fall.

spring
Spring is the season that follows winter.

summer
Summer is the season that follows spring.

fall

Fall is the season that follows summer.

Start with Your Standards

Standard Set 3. Earth Sciences

3.a. *Students know* how to use simple tools (e.g., thermometer, wind vane) to measure weather conditions and record changes from day to day and across the seasons.

3.b. *Students know* that weather changes from day to day but that trends in temperature or rain (or snow) tend to be predictable during a season.

3.c. *Students know* the sun warms the land, air, and water.

Standards Set 4. Investigation and Experimentation covered in this chapter: 4.a., 4.b., 4.c.

What Is Winter Weather?

Building Background

Winter is the coldest season. It snows in some places and is warm in other places.

Inquiry Skill

Classify Group objects that are alike in some way.

 STANDARDS

3.b. *Students know* that the weather changes from day to day but that trends in temperature or rain (or snow) tend to be predictable during a season.
4.a. Draw pictures that portray some features of the thing being described.

What You Need

spinner

paper squares

crayons

paper

What to Wear

Steps

1. Take turns spinning the spinner.

2. **Communicate** Name a clothing item you might wear when the air is that temperature. Draw the item you name.

3. **Classify** Sort the clothing pictures by warm or cool temperatures. Label each group.

Think and Share

1. **Compare** How are all the warm weather clothes you drew alike?

2. What clothes keep you warm in cool weather?

STEP 1

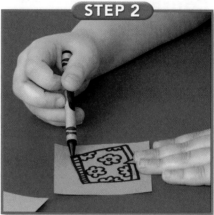
STEP 2

STEP 3

Guided Inquiry

Ask Questions Suppose you are going to visit a different place in winter. Ask questions to **infer** what clothes you should pack.

🎯 **Reading Skill**

Cause and Effect

📖 **STANDARDS**

3.b. *Students know* that the weather changes from day to day but that trends in temperature or rain (or snow) tend to be predictable during a season.

3.a. *Students know* how to use simple tools (e.g., thermometer, wind vane) to measure weather conditions and record changes from day to day and across the seasons.

Winter

A **season** is a time of year that has its own kind of weather. **Winter** is the season that follows fall.

Winter is the coldest season of the year. The temperature gets colder because there is less sunlight in winter.

Sweet Gum Tree in Winter

Leaves and fruit fall. The tree rests.

Why is it hard for animals to find food here?

Sometimes it is hard for animals to find food in winter. In cold weather, many plants stop growing. Some plants die. Others only rest. Some plants are covered with snow.

🎯 **Cause and Effect** What happens to weather when there is less sunlight?

Express Lab

Activity Card 18
Show Winter Weather

Winter in Different Places

Winter weather is different in different places. Winter is very cold in some places. Winter is only a little cooler than summer in other places. Some places have wet winters. Other places have dry winters.

🎯 **Cause and Effect** Why do people go to the beach during the winter in some places?

WASHINGTON

OREGON

IDA

NEVADA

A

CALIFORNIA

San Joaquin, California

Rain keeps the grass green in winter.

Santa Barbara, California

People still play on the beach in winter.

Washburn, North Dakota

Cold weather brings snow and ice.

Lesson Wrap-Up

❶ **Vocabulary** What is **winter**?

❷ 🎯 **Reading Skill** What happens to plants when the weather gets cooler?

❸ **Classify** What can a thermometer tell you about winter in different places?

💻 **Technology** Visit **www.eduplace.com/cascp** to find out more about winter.

STANDARDS 1–2: 3.b., 3: 3.a.

What Is Spring Weather?

Building Background

The temperature begins to get warmer in spring. New plants begin to grow.

Inquiry Skill

Communicate **Share with others what you learn and observe.**

 STANDARDS

3.b. *Students know* that the weather changes from day to day but that trends in temperature or rain (or snow) tend to be predictable during a season.
4.b. Record observations and data with pictures, numbers, or written statements.

What You Need

2 cups

paper towels

seeds

water

Grow Plants

Steps

STEP 1

1. Spray water on the paper towels. Fill each cup with paper towels.

2. Add seeds to each cup.

STEP 2

3. **Predict** Put the **winter** cup in a cold place. Put the **spring** cup in a warm place. Tell what you think will happen.

4. **Communicate** Look at the seeds after five days. Write about how they have changed.

STEP 3

Think and Share

1. What helped the seeds grow?

2. **Infer** Do plants grow better in winter or in spring?

Guided Inquiry

Experiment Put the sprouted seeds in soil. Make a plan for caring for the plants. **Observe** the plants for one month.

189

▶ **Vocabulary**

spring

🎯 **Reading Skill**

Main Idea and Details

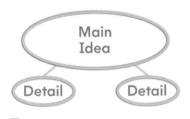

Main Idea

Detail   Detail

STANDARDS

3.b. *Students know* that the weather changes from day to day but that trends in temperature or rain (or snow) tend to be predictable during a season.
3.a. *Students know* how to use simple tools (e.g., thermometer, wind vane) to measure weather conditions and record changes from day to day and across the seasons.

Spring

Spring is the season that follows winter. Weather begins to get warmer in spring. There is more light from the Sun in spring than in winter. Warmer weather, rain, and more daylight help plants grow in spring.

In many places, spring is rainy.

Many new plants grow in spring. New plants make it easy for animals to find food. Many baby animals are born in warm spring weather.

goose with gosling

🎯 **Main Idea** How can you tell it is spring?

Sweet Gum Tree in Spring

New leaves begin to grow. Flowers bloom.

Express Lab

Activity Card 19
Find the Best Place to Grow Plants

191

Spring in Different Places

Spring weather is different in different places. Places that were very cold in winter may be cool in spring. Spring may be warmer in places that did not have a cold winter.

Main Idea How can spring weather be different in different places?

WASHINGTON

OREGON

IDAH

NEVADA

A

CALIFORNIA

Mount Shasta, California

Spring weather is cool in these mountains.

Borrego Springs, California

Spring weather is warm in the desert.

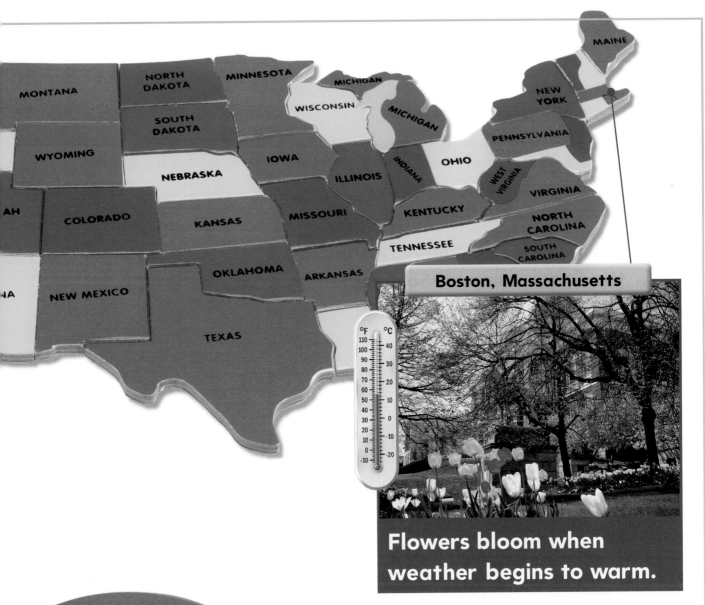

MAINE

MONTANA

NORTH DAKOTA

MINNESOTA

MICHIGAN

NEW YORK

WISCONSIN

MICHIGAN

PENNSYLVANIA

WYOMING

SOUTH DAKOTA

IOWA

OHIO

INDIANA

WEST VIRGINIA

VIRGINIA

NEBRASKA

ILLINOIS

AH

COLORADO

KANSAS

MISSOURI

KENTUCKY

NORTH CAROLINA

TENNESSEE

SOUTH CAROLINA

NA

NEW MEXICO

OKLAHOMA

ARKANSAS

Boston, Massachusetts

TEXAS

Flowers bloom when weather begins to warm.

Lesson Wrap-Up

❶ **Vocabulary** What is **spring**?

❷ 🎯 **Reading Skill** Tell three things you know about spring.

❸ **Communicate** Tell how thermometers can help you understand spring weather.

 **Technology** Visit **www.eduplace.com/cascp** to find out more about spring.

STANDARDS 1–2: 3.b., 3: 3.a.

What Is Summer Weather?

Building Background

We get the most light from the Sun in summer. So summer is the warmest season.

Inquiry Skill

Observe Use your senses to learn about things around you.

sun-and-shade chart

STANDARDS

3.c. *Students know* the sun warms the land, air, and water.
4.b. Record observations and data with pictures, numbers, or written statements.

Sun and Shade

Steps

STEP 1

1. Go outside. Find something that is partly in the Sun and partly in the shade.

2. **Observe** Touch the part that is in the Sun. Record how warm or cool it feels.

STEP 2

3. **Observe** Touch the part that is in the shade. Record what you observe.

4. Do steps 1–3 with different things. **Safety:** Do not touch hot metal things!

STEP 3

Think and Share

1. **Compare** How are things in the Sun different from things in the shade?

2. **Infer** Why do people look for shady places in summer?

Guided Inquiry

Experiment Try the experiment on another day. Are your results the same or different? **Infer** why that happened.

Vocabulary

summer

⊚ **Reading Skill**

Compare and Contrast

Compare	Contrast

▎ **STANDARDS**

3.b. *Students know* that the weather changes from day to day but that trends in temperature or rain (or snow) tend to be predictable during a season.
3.c. *Students know* the sun warms the land, air, and water.

Summer

Summer is the season that follows spring. Summer is the warmest season of the year. It gets the most light from the Sun. Land, air, and water get warm when the Sun shines on them.

This girl is enjoying warm summer weather.

Plants grow in the warm summer weather. Young animals also grow in summer. They learn to find their own food.

🎯 **Compare and Contrast**
How are spring and summer different?

Growing plants are food for the lamb.

Sweet Gum Tree in Summer

Spiny fruits form.

Express Lab

Activity Card 20
Show Summer Weather

Summer in Different Places

Summer weather is different in different places. Some places have little rain in summer. Other places have a lot of rain. People and animals look for shade on hot summer days.

◎ Compare and Contrast
In which place is summer the warmest?

WASHINGTON

OREGON

NEVADA

CALIFORNIA

San Francisco, California

People often wear sweaters in summer.

Monterey, California

Grass turns brown when there is no rain.

Miami, Florida

Shade helps people feel cooler in hot weather.

Lesson Wrap-Up

1. **Vocabulary** What is **summer**?

2. **Reading Skill** How does the temperature change from spring to summer?

3. **Observe** How can you use your senses to tell how the Sun warms land, air, and water?

 Technology Visit **www.eduplace.com/cascp** to find out more about summer.

STANDARDS 1–2: 3.b., 3: 3.c.

Dry Days of Summer

It's summer! It's hot! People, plants, and animals need water. We get water from rain. But what happens when there is little rain?

Most of California has little rain in summer. So people find ways to use less water. Here are some things you and your family can do.

The land is dry because there is little rain.

STANDARDS

3.b. *Students know* that weather changes from day to day but that trends in temperature or of rain (or snow) tend to be predictable during a season.
3.c. *Students know* that the sun warms the land, air, and water.

READING **LINK**

Ways to Use Less Water

Water gardens at the end of the day when the Sun cannot dry up the water.

Use a broom instead of water to clean a sidewalk.

Turn off the water when you are not using it.

Sharing Ideas

1. **Write About It** Think about how you use water. Write ways that you could use less water.

2. **Talk About It** Why do we need rainy weather?

What Is Fall Weather?

Building Background

Fall follows summer. The weather begins to get cooler.

Inquiry Skill

Record Data You can show what you observe on a bar graph.

 STANDARDS

3.b. *Students know* that the weather changes from day to day but that trends in temperature or rain (or snow) tend to be predictable during a season.
4.c. Record observations on a bar graph.

What You Need

Temperatures in Lemoore	
Season	Temperature
Winter	45° F
Spring	60° F
Summer	80° F
Fall	65° F

temperature chart

marker

bar graph

Fall Weather

Steps

① Look at the temperature chart. Write the season names in order on the bottom of the bar graph.

STEP 1

② **Record Data** Color a bar to show the temperature in winter. Then color a bar for each other season.

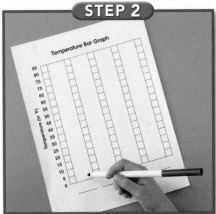

STEP 2

③ **Compare** the temperatures in these four seasons.

STEP 3

Think and Share

1. **Use Data** Which season has the warmest weather?

2. How does the temperature change from season to season?

Guided Inquiry

Experiment Record the temperature where you live at the beginning of each month. **Communicate** what you find.

Vocabulary
fall

Reading Skill

Sequence

Step 1

Step 2

Step 3

STANDARDS

3.b. *Students know* that the weather changes from day to day but that trends in temperature or rain (or snow) tend to be predictable during a season.

Fall

Fall is the season that follows summer. There are fewer hours of sunlight in fall than in summer.

The weather gets cooler in fall. People wear warmer clothes. Some leaves change color and fall to the ground.

In fall, animals get ready for cold weather. Some animals grow thicker fur to keep warm. Many animals store food for winter.

Many plants change as the air gets cooler. Farm crops die.

A squirrel stores food for winter.

Sequence What season comes after summer?

Sweet Gum Tree in Fall

Leaves turn red and fall off.

Express Lab

Activity Card 21
Classify Leaves

Fall in Different Places

After summer, the weather begins to get cooler. But fall weather is different in different places. Some places are warmer than others. Fall is a rainy season in some places.

Sequence What happens to the temperature from summer to fall?

WASHINGTON

OREGON

ID

NEVADA

CALIFORNIA

Paradise, California

The rainy season starts in fall.

Bishop, California

Leaves turn color in fall weather.

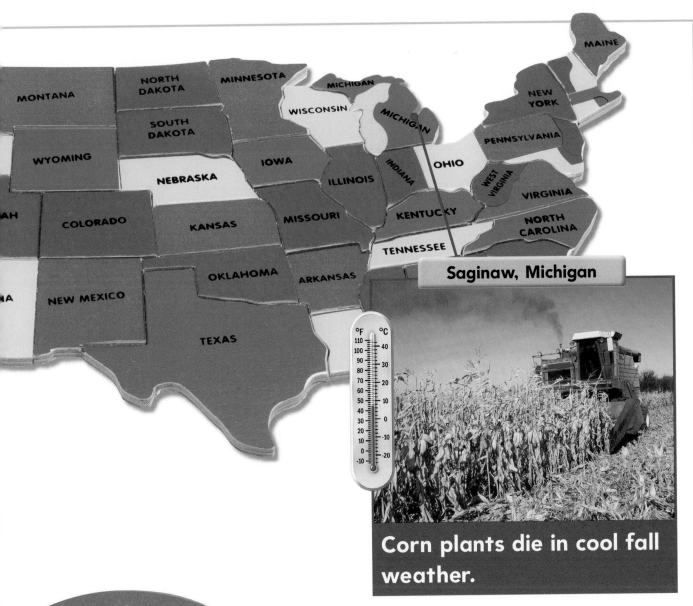

Saginaw, Michigan

Corn plants die in cool fall weather.

 Lesson Wrap-Up

❶ **Vocabulary** What is **fall**?

❷ 🎯 **Reading Skill** Which season comes after fall?

❸ **Record Data** How can a bar graph help you compare temperatures?

📱 **Technology** Visit **www.eduplace.com/cascp** to find out more about fall.

EXTREME Science

So Hot! So Cold!

Freezing cold? Burning hot? No problem! These animals do just fine living in some of the coldest winters and hottest summers on Earth.

◀ **Ouch! This lizard lives in a California desert. Its scaly skin protects it from the desert heat.**

▼ **Brrrr! Penguins live where the weather is icy cold. Layers of fat and thick feathers protect penguins from the cold.**

My Journal

Do you think a penguin and a lizard could live in a place with the same weather? Write your ideas in your journal.

209

Math Read a Bar Graph

Ms. Lane's class made a bar graph to show rainfall in different months.

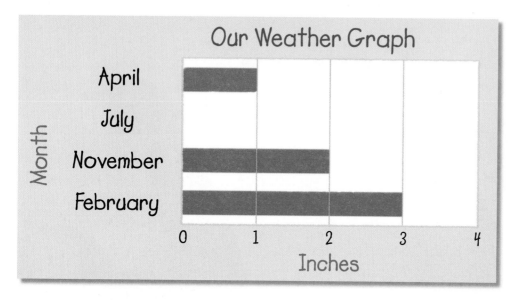

Our Weather Graph

1. How much rain fell in July?

2. Which month had the most rain?

Writing Describe a Place

Winter is cold in many places. But winter is warm or hot in some places. Tell about winter where you live. Draw a picture of yourself in winter.

Winter is warm where I live.

A. G. Kawamura

A. G. Kawamura works for the state of California. His job is to help farmers grow and sell crops.

In most of California, crops grow all year long. Different crops grow best in different seasons.

Visual Summary

Weather changes from season to season.

Winter

Winter is the coolest season.

Spring

Spring weather begins to get warmer.

Fall

Fall weather begins to get cooler.

Summer

Summer is the warmest season.

My Journal

Review your answers to the Lesson Preview questions.

STANDARDS 3.a., 3.b., 3.c.

Main Ideas

1. What is a season? (p. 184)

2. What happens to land, water, and air in summer? (p. 196)

3. How does weather change from summer to fall? (p. 204)

Vocabulary

Choose the correct word from the box.

4. the warmest season

5. the season that follows winter

6. the season when weather starts to get cooler

fall (p. 204)
spring (p. 190)
summer (p. 196)
winter (p. 184)

7. the season that has the coolest weather

Using Science Skills

8. Use the chart to make a bar graph.

9. **Critical Thinking** How can weather tools help you explain fall weather?

Winter	
Month	Degrees
December	5°F
January	5°F
February	10°F

STANDARDS 1: 3.b., 2: 3.c., 3–7: 3.b., 8: 4.c., 9: 3.a.

Test Practice

Choose the correct answer.

1. What does this tool measure?

rain	wind	temperature
○	○	○

2. Air can be warmed by _____.

clouds	the Sun	a thermometer
○	○	○

3. Which thermometer shows the temperature in a cold season?

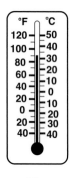 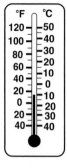 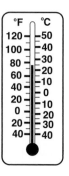

   ○   ○   ○

4. Which is a kind of weather?

rainy   the Sun   temperature

○   ○   ○

5. Each year spring follows _____.

summer   fall   winter

○   ○   ○

Checking Main Ideas

Write the correct answer.

6. Tell how weather changes from season to season.

7. Write about what the Sun is warming in this picture.

STANDARDS 1: 3.a., 2: 3.c., 3: 3.a., 4–6: 3.b., 7: 3.c.

You Can...

Discover More

Why doesn't it snow everywhere in winter?

During winter, the Sun is higher in the sky in places nearer the Equator. These places get more direct light and heat from the Sun all year. During winter, it is usually too warm to snow in these places.

winter in California

winter in Florida

 Simulations Go to **www.eduplace.com/cascp** to see why it snows in some places during winter.

PHYSICAL  SCIENCE

UNIT D

Materials and Their Forms

California Connection

Visit www.eduplace.com/cascp
to find out more about matter.

Let's Go!

The Watts Towers

The towers are decorated with seashells, colored glass, and broken dishes.

The Watts Towers are made of steel bars, wrapped in wire and covered with cement.

The walls surrounding the towers are decorated in the front and back.

Materials and Their Forms

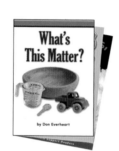

Statue of Liberty

California Big Idea!

Standard Set 1.
Physical Sciences

Materials come in different forms (states), including solids, liquids, and gases.

Solids, Liquids, and Gases

Solids, liquids, gases are the
  forms that matter takes.
They can be broken, heated,
  frozen, and evaporate.

A solid has its shape, but you
  can do something to it.
You can bend it, or tear it,
  or even glue it.

 from *Science Songs*, track 20

Chapter 7

Solids, Liquids, and Gases

Ice sculptures

LESSON 1

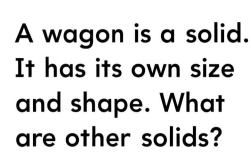

A wagon is a solid. It has its own size and shape. What are other solids?

LESSON 2

Orange juice is a liquid. How can you tell that something is a liquid?

LESSON 3

Air is a gas that you cannot see. How can you tell which tire is filled with air?

My Journal

Write or draw in your journal to answer the questions above.

Vocabulary

Picture Glossary

Vocabulary Skill

Find All the Meanings

matter

You might ask, "What's the matter with that car?" **Matter** means "trouble." The word **matter** also means "what all things are made of."

solid
A solid is matter that has its own size and shape.

liquid
A liquid is matter that flows and takes the shape of its container.

gas
A gas is matter that spreads out to fill all the space it is in.

Start with Your Standards

Standard Set 1. Physical Sciences

1.a. *Students know* solids, liquids, and gases have different properties.

Standard Set 4. Investigation and Experimentation covered in this chapter: 4.b., 4.d., 4.e.

matter

Matter is what all things are made of. It can be a solid, a liquid, or a gas.

What Are Solids?

Building Background

All things are made of matter. A solid is a kind of matter that has its own size and shape.

Inquiry Skill

Observe Use your senses to learn about things around you.

paper

pencil

STANDARDS

1.a. *Students know* solids, liquids, and gases have different properties.
4.d. Describe the relative position of objects by using two references (e.g., above and next to, below and left of).

Find Solids

Steps

1 **Observe** List five objects that have shapes that do not change.

STEP 1

2 **Communicate** Choose one object. Use two clues such as **above the book** and **next to the ball** to tell how to find it.

STEP 2

3 Ask a partner to find the object.

4 Give clues for other objects.

STEP 3

Think and Share

1. What are some words you used to tell where the objects were?

2. **Compare** How are solids alike and different?

Guided Inquiry

Experiment Use a hand lens to **observe** a solid. Tell what you can see with the hand lens that you cannot see without it.

🎯 **Reading Skill**

Classify

Group	Group	Group

STANDARDS

1.a. *Students know* solids, liquids, and gases have different properties.

Solids

Matter is what all things are made of. Solids, liquids, and gases are all matter.

A **solid** is matter that has its own size and shape. Rocks and bikes are solids.

A solid keeps its shape until you do something to change it. You can cut, bend, or break a solid to change its shape.

Classify **What are three things that are solids?**

What solids do you see in this picture?

Properties of Solids

Different solids have different properties. Color, shape, size, and texture are **properties**. A balloon can be red or yellow. Slippers can be soft and fuzzy. Pencils can be made of wood or plastic.

Which objects are soft?
Which objects are smooth?

Other properties tell what solids do. Clay can stretch and bend. Crayons can break. Plastic blocks float in water. Rocks sink. Some solids let light through.

Classify What are properties you can see?

Lesson Wrap-Up

❶ **Vocabulary** What is **matter**?

❷ **Reading Skill** What are three properties of solids?

❸ **Observe** How can you use your senses to describe a solid?

Technology Visit **www.eduplace.com/cascp** to find out more about solids.

STANDARDS 1–3: 1.a.

STANDARDS 1.a. *Students know* solids, liquids, and gases have different properties.

Almost Not There!

Why aren't those crayons melting? Look closely. The crayons are sitting on something called aerogel. Aerogel is the lightest solid in the world. It's mostly air! Aerogel is used to protect objects from extreme heat and cold.

It would take a cube of aerogel 2 meters tall to balance a six-year-old's weight!

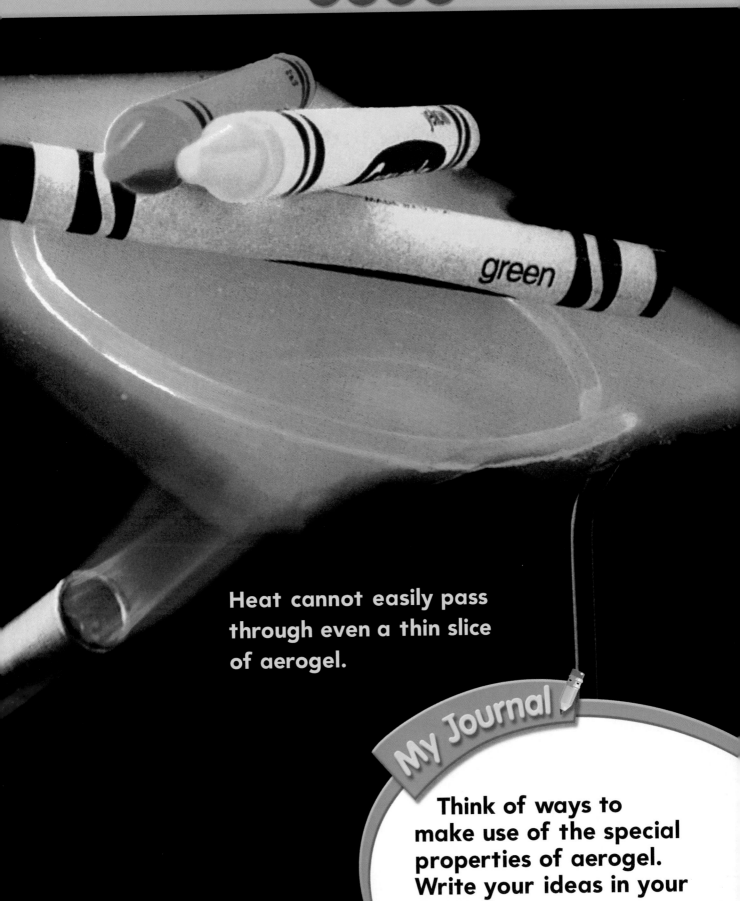

Heat cannot easily pass through even a thin slice of aerogel.

My Journal

Think of ways to make use of the special properties of aerogel. Write your ideas in your journal.

231

What Are Liquids?

Building Background

Liquids can change shape. A liquid flows and takes the shape of its container.

Inquiry Skill

Compare Look for ways that objects are alike and different.

 STANDARDS

1.a. *Students know* solids, liquids, and gases have different properties.
4.e. Make new observations when discrepancies exist between two descriptions of the same object or phenomenon.

What You Need

water

measuring cup

containers

paper and crayons

Compare Liquids

Steps

1 **Measure** Put half a cup of water into a measuring cup. Observe the water's shape. Draw what you see.

2 **Observe** Pour the water into other containers. Look at the water's shape. Draw what you see each time.

3 Share your drawings. If you had different ideas, try pouring the liquids again.

STEP 1

STEP 2

STEP 3

Think and Share

1. **Compare** How was the water in each container alike? How was it different?

2. **Infer** What are some properties of water?

Guided Inquiry

Experiment Pour different liquids, such as honey and cooking oil, into containers. **Compare** how the liquids flow.

► **Vocabulary**

liquid

◎ **Reading Skill**

Compare and Contrast

Compare	Contrast

▲ **STANDARDS**

1.a. *Students know* solids, liquids, and gases have different properties.

Liquids

You can pour water. You can pour milk and juice. Water, milk, and juice are liquids. A **liquid** is matter that flows and takes the shape of its container.

How can you change the shape of a liquid?

A solid has its own shape. A liquid does not have its own shape. Its shape changes as it flows. A liquid does not always fill its container.

raindrops on a leaf

🎯 **Compare** How are solids and liquids different?

Ocean water is a liquid.

Express Lab

Activity Card 23
Compare How Liquids Flow

Comparing Liquids

Different liquids may have different properties. Liquids may be different colors. Milk is white. Grape juice is purple. Liquids may also feel different. Honey feels sticky. Cooking oil feels slippery.

Orange juice pours quickly.

Honey pours slowly.

Liquids can taste different.
Lemon juice tastes sour.
Apple juice tastes sweet.
Liquids also smell different.
Perfume may smell like
flowers. Clean water has
no smell at all.

**One property
of water is
that you can
see through it.**

**Compare How are the
properties of milk and honey
different?**

Lesson Wrap-Up

❶ **Vocabulary** What is a **liquid**?

❷ **Reading Skill** What happens if you
pour the same amount of water into two
containers of different shapes?

❸ **Compare** How are solids and liquids
different?

Technology Visit **www.eduplace.com/cascp** to
find out more about liquids.

STANDARDS 1–3: 1.a.

Water Clocks

All day long people ask, "What time is it?" Long ago, people asked the same question. They did not have watches. They knew the properties of water. So they made water clocks.

Water drips from this clock. To tell time, people matched the water level with lines on the side.

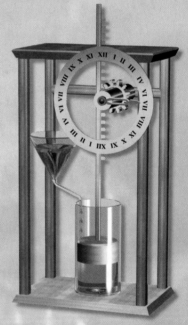

Water fills the lower container. The water raises a stick. The stick turns the clock's hands.

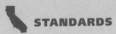

STANDARDS
1.a. *Students know* solids, liquids, and gases have different properties.

READING LINK

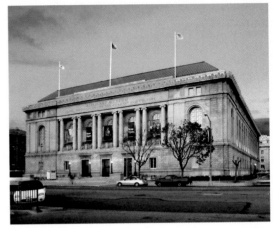

There is a very old water clock at the Asian Art Museum in San Francisco.

Su Song of China made a water clock like this. It was as tall as a three-story building.

Sharing Ideas

1. **Write About It** How does a water clock use the properties of liquids?

2. **Talk About It** What problems might you have if you used a water clock?

What Are Gases?

Building Background

Gas is matter that changes shape to fill the space it is in. The air you breathe is a gas.

Inquiry Skill

Experiment Make a plan, choosing the items to use and the steps to follow.

What You Need

goggles

balloon

paper and pencil

STANDARDS

1.a. *Students know* solids, liquids, and gases have different properties.
4.b. Record observations and data with pictures, numbers, or written statements.

Gas Shapes

Steps

1 **Communicate** Talk about what is inside the balloon.
Safety: Wear goggles!

STEP 1

2 **Experiment** Carefully squeeze the balloon into different shapes. Watch what happens to the shape.

STEP 2

3 **Record Data** Write a sentence to tell what happened to the air in the balloon.

STEP 3

Think and Share

1. What happened to the air in the balloon?

2. **Infer** What will happen to the air in the balloon if you untie the balloon?

Guided Inquiry

Experiment Use scissors or a pin to make a small opening in the balloon's knot. **Observe** what happens to the balloon.

Vocabulary

gas

Reading Skill
**Main Idea
and Details**

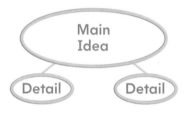

STANDARDS

1.a. *Students know* solids, liquids, and gases
have different properties.

Gases

A liquid will take the shape of the container it is in. But a liquid may not fill all of a container.

A **gas** is matter that spreads out to fill all the space it is in. A gas always fills a closed container. The gas can come out when a container is opened.

Air fills the bubble. Air is a gas.

A gas spreads out to fill a balloon.

Gases are all around you. The air that you breathe is a gas. When you blow up a balloon, you fill it with gas. You cannot see the gas. You can feel the gas when you let it out.

Main Idea What are the properties of a gas?

Express Lab

Activity Card 24
Observe Air

Comparing Gases

Different gases can do different things. Living things use air to stay alive. Some gases are used to cook food. One kind of gas can heat a home. Another kind of gas can make a balloon rise.

Main Idea What kind of gas do living things need to stay alive?

Heat from a burning gas cooks the food.

Helium gas fills
these balloons.

Lesson Wrap-Up

❶ **Vocabulary** What is a **gas**?

❷ 🎯 **Reading Skill** What are some ways people use gas?

❸ **Experiment** How can doing an experiment help you understand the properties of gases?

💻 **Technology** Visit **www.eduplace.com/cascp** to find out more about gases.

STANDARDS 1–3: 1.a.

Math Count Matter

Make a tally chart to show the number of solids, liquids, and gases in the picture. Some solids may contain a liquid or a gas.

1. Which form of matter is found most often in the picture?

2. How many more solids are there than liquids?

Writing Describe a Place

What is your favorite place? Tell about the solids, liquids, and gases that are in your favorite place.

Chemist

Chemists work with solids, liquids, and gases. They study the properties of matter and how matter changes.

Some chemists try to invent new materials. Chemists might help make water cleaner. They might make car tires stronger.

What It Takes!

- A college degree in chemistry
- Good math skills
- Hard work and patience

Visual Summary

Matter is all around you. It can be a solid, a liquid, or a gas.

Properties of Matter

A solid has its own size and shape.	A liquid does not have its own shape.	A gas fills all the space it is in.

My Journal

Review your answers to the Lesson Preview questions.

STANDARDS 1.a.

Main Ideas

1. How can you tell that an object is a solid? (p. 226)

2. How do you know that water, milk, and juice are not solids? (p. 234)

3. How is a gas different from a liquid? (p. 242)

Vocabulary

Choose the correct word from the box.

4. What all things are made of

5. Color, shape, size, and texture

6. Matter that flows and takes the shape of its container

7. Matter that fills the space it is in

gas (p. 242)
liquid (p. 234)
matter (p. 226)
properties (p. 228)

Using Science Skills

8. Choose a solid in your classroom. Use two clues to tell where it is.

9. **Critical Thinking** Is clay a solid? Why?

Chapter 8

Changes in Materials

Merced River in
Yosemite National Park

LESSON 1

A crayon may get soft if it is left in the Sun. Why does that happen?

LESSON 2

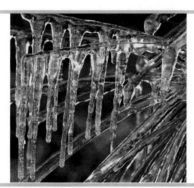

You may see icicles when it is cold. What are they made of?

LESSON 3

A fruit salad is a mixture. What other mixtures do you eat?

LESSON 4

Many people eat popcorn. Can popcorn be unpopped? Why?

My Journal

Write or draw in your journal to answer the questions above.

Vocabulary

Picture Glossary

Vocabulary Skill

Use Opposites

melt   freeze

Hot and **cold** are opposites. **Melt** and **freeze** are opposites. How are **melt** and **freeze** different?

melt

To melt is to change from a solid to a liquid.

freeze

To freeze is to change from a liquid to a solid.

mixture

A mixture is two or more kinds of matter put together.

Start with Your Standards

Standard Set 1. Physical Sciences

1.a. *Students know* solids, liquids, and gases have different properties.

1.b. *Students know* the properties of substances can change when the substances are mixed, cooled, or heated.

Standard Set 3. Earth Sciences

3.c. *Students know* the sun warms the land, air, and water.

Standard Set 4. Investigation and Experimentation covered in this chapter: 4.a., 4.b., 4.c.

heat

Heat is a kind of energy that makes things warm.

What Does Heating Do?

Building Background

Heating matter can change its properties. It can change solids to liquids or liquids to gases.

Inquiry Skill

Predict Use what you know to tell what you think will happen.

STANDARDS

1.b. *Students know* the properties of substances can change when the substances are mixed, cooled, or heated.
4.c. Record observations on a bar graph.

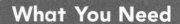

bag of ice

thermometer

warm water

bar graph and marker

Heating Ice

Steps

STEP 1

1. **Measure** Put a thermometer in a bag of ice. Record the temperature on a bar graph.

STEP 2

2. **Predict** Put the bag of ice in a bowl of warm water. Tell what you think will happen to the ice.

3. **Record Data** Wait one hour. Record the temperature on the bar graph.

STEP 3

4. Repeat Step 3.

Think and Share

1. **Communicate** Show your bar graph to a classmate. Tell how the temperature changed.

2. **Infer** Why did the temperature change?

Guided Inquiry

Experiment What does heat do to other solids? Repeat the experiment with butter. **Compare** your results.

▶ **Vocabulary**

energy
heat
melt
evaporate

🎯 **Reading Skill**
Cause and Effect

Cause ➡ Effect

⬥ STANDARDS

1.b. *Students know* the properties of substances can change when the substances are mixed, cooled, or heated.
3.c. *Students know* the sun warms the land, air, and water.

Heat

Energy is the power to cause change. **Heat** is a kind of energy that makes things warm. Heat from the Sun warms Earth's land, air, and water.

Express Lab

Activity Card 25
Feel Heat

Heat comes from other places, too. Fire gives off heat. So do a lit stove and a burning candle. Rubbing things together can make them give off heat, too.

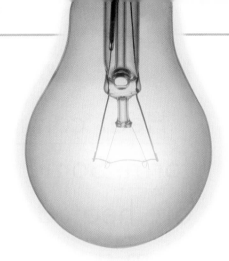

Light bulbs can get very hot.

🎯 **Cause and Effect** How does heat from the Sun change things?

What happens when you rub your hands together?

Heat warms your home.

Heat Changes Solids to Liquids

Heat can make matter change form. Some solids melt when they are heated. To **melt** is to change from a solid to a liquid.

Ice is a solid. Ice melts when it gets warm. The ice changes from a solid to a liquid.

Heat can melt
a juice bar.

Why are the candles melting?

Heat Changes Liquids to Gases

Heat can make a liquid evaporate. To **evaporate** is to change from a liquid to a gas. Water evaporates when it is heated. You cannot see water when it is a gas.

Heat from the Sun made the puddles evaporate.

 **Cause and Effect** How can heat change water?

Lesson Wrap-Up

❶ **Vocabulary** What is **heat**?

❷  **Reading Skill** What kind of energy causes a liquid to evaporate?

❸ **Predict** What would happen to ice cream if you left it outside on a sunny day?

Technology Visit **www.eduplace.com/cascp** to find out more about how heat changes things.

STANDARDS **1.b.** *Students know* the properties of substances can change when the substances are mixed, cooled, or heated.

Sand to Glass

What can you do with sand?
If you have enough heat, you can change sand into glass!

Glassmakers put sand into a very hot oven. The oven melts the sand. The sand turns into a stretchy goo. The goo can then be molded and shaped. As the goo cools, it hardens and turns into solid, smooth glass!

Most glass begins as sand just like the kind you find at beaches.

Dale Chihuly is a glass artist. He made these beautiful glass balls. He begins with pure white sand and then adds colors when the sand melts.

My Journal

Think about other kinds of matter that melt when heated and become a solid when cooled. Make a list for your journal.

261

What Does Cooling Do?

Building Background

Cooling can change the properties of matter. A liquid can change to a solid if it gets very cold.

Inquiry Skill

Use Numbers Use numbers to describe and compare objects or events.

What You Need

cup

water

ruler

paper and pencil

 STANDARDS

1.b. *Students know* the properties of substances can change when the substances are mixed, cooled, or heated.
4.b. Record observations and data with pictures, numbers, or written statements.

Cooling Water

Steps

STEP 1

1 **Measure** Pour water into a cup. Use a ruler to measure the height of the water. Record the data.

STEP 2

2 **Experiment** Place the cup of water in a freezer overnight. Measure the height of the water the next day. Record the data.

STEP 3

3 **Record Data** Wait three hours. Measure the water again. Record your data.

Think and Share

1. What happened to the water in the freezer?

2. **Use Numbers** Did the amount of water change during the experiment? Explain.

Guided Inquiry

Experiment Put different liquids into containers. **Measure** the liquids. Freeze them. Then measure again. Compare the measurements.

Vocabulary

freeze

Reading Skill

Draw Conclusions

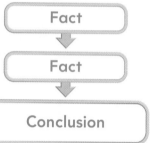

Fact

↓

Fact

↓

Conclusion

STANDARDS

1.b. *Students know* the properties of substances can change when the substances are mixed, cooled, or heated.
1.a. *Students know* solids, liquids, and gases have different properties.

Cooling

Cooling happens when heat is taken away. Air gets cooler when the Sun goes down.

Cooling can make matter change forms. It can make liquids freeze. To **freeze** is to change from a liquid to a solid.

Which is colder, the juice or the ice?

A Pond Changes

Fall
The water in the pond is liquid.

Winter
The water on the top of the pond is solid.

In winter, the temperature drops. The air and water are cold. The water in a pond changes from a liquid to a solid.

Draw Conclusions Why does a pond freeze in winter?

Express Lab

Activity Card 26
Observe Ice

Cooling Changes Gases

Cooling makes gases change to liquids. When water is a gas, it is water vapor. There is water vapor in your breath. On a cold day, water vapor in your breath changes to a liquid.

Cold air changes water vapor in the animal's breath from a gas to a liquid.

The air outside the glass is warm. The ice in the glass is cold. Drops of water form when water vapor in the air cools near the glass.

Draw Conclusions Why do drops of water form when you breathe on a cold window?

Why are these glasses wet on the outside?

Lesson Wrap-Up

❶ **Vocabulary** How does water change when you **freeze** it?

❷ **Reading Skill** How could you cool a hot bowl of soup? Why would your idea work?

❸ **Use Numbers** How does using numbers help you learn more about cooling things?

Technology Visit **www.eduplace.com/cascp** to find out more about cooling.

STANDARDS 1: 1.a., 1.b., 2: 1.b., 3: 4.b.

What Happens When You Mix Things?

Building Background

Solids, liquids, and gases can be mixed. You make a mixture when you put fruit and milk on cereal.

Inquiry Skill

Communicate Share with others what you learn and observe.

What You Need

bowl

spoon

warm water

salt

 STANDARDS

1.b. *Students know* the properties of substances can change when the substances are mixed, cooled, or heated.
4.b. Record observations and data with pictures, numbers, or written statements.

Make a Mixture

Steps

1. Put salt in a bowl. Add water to the bowl.

2. Stir. Tell how the mixture looks. **Safety:** Do not taste the mixture!

3. **Observe** Put the mixture in a warm place. Look at what happens after a few days.

STEP 1

STEP 2

STEP 3

Think and Share

1. What happened to the salt?

2. **Communicate** Write what you learned about the mixture. Share it with others.

Guided Inquiry

Experiment Try mixing other things with water. You might use solids or other liquids. **Communicate** what you observe to a partner.

▶ **Vocabulary**

mixture

dissolve

🎯 **Reading Skill**

Main Idea and Details

Main Idea

Detail   Detail

STANDARDS

1.b. *Students know* the properties of substances can change when the substances are mixed, cooled, or heated.

Solid Mixtures

A **mixture** is two or more kinds of matter put together. Some mixtures are all solids. You have a mixture when you make a sandwich.

What are the solids that make up this mixture?

Mixtures can be taken apart. You can take parts off your sandwich. You can use a magnet to pull iron or steel from some mixtures. You can use water to see what parts of a mixture float.

Main Idea How can you make a mixture?

Express Lab

Activity Card 27
Make a Mixture

Mixing Solids and Liquids

You can make a mixture with solids and liquids. Some solids **dissolve**, or mix completely, in water. Sugar dissolves in water. You cannot see it, but it is there.

A drink mix dissolves in water.

Mixing Liquids and Gases

You can mix a liquid and a gas. A fish tank has a mixture of liquid and gas. The water in the tank is a liquid. The bubbles are air. Air is a gas.

Air bubbles mix with the water.

 **Main Idea** What happens to sugar when you mix it in water?

![target icon] **Lesson Wrap-Up**

❶ **Vocabulary** What is a **mixture**?

❷ ![target icon] **Reading Skill** Are toys in a toy box a mixture? Tell why or why not.

❸ **Communicate** List three mixtures that you see in your classroom. Share your ideas with a classmate.

![computer icon] **Technology** Visit **www.eduplace.com/cascp** to find out more about mixtures.

Cooking Contest

Cast

Judge

Chef 1

Chef 2

Chef 3

STANDARD

1.b. *Students know* the properties of substances can change when the substances are mixed, cooled or heated.

READING **LINK**

Judge: Welcome to the Cooking Contest. Chef 1, tell me about what you made.

Chef 1: Judge, I made lasagna! I put hard noodles in hot water. The heat and the water made the noodles soft.

Judge: What did you do next?

Chef 1: I mixed liquid tomato sauce with the noodles. I added meat, cheese, and vegetables.

Judge: It sounds delicious! May I try a bite? [The judge tastes.] Yum! This is delicious.

Judge: Chef 2, what did you make?

Chef 2: I made peach cobbler. I heated a mixture of peaches, sugar, and cinnamon. The heat made the peaches soft. It melted the sugar.

Judge: May I try it?

Chef 2: Yes! But first, I will put ice cream on top. The heat from the cobbler will melt the ice cream.

Judge: [tasting] This is great!

Judge: Chef 3, it is your turn.

Chef 3: I made cold green pea and mint soup.

Judge: I thought soups were hot.

Chef 3: The soup starts hot, but I cool it. I melt butter. Then I mix in onions, peas, mint, and milk. Last, I put the soup in the refrigerator. Have a taste.

Judge: What a mixture! Now, I must choose a winner.

Sharing Ideas

1. **Write About It** Choose a winner. List ways the winning chef used heating, cooling, and mixing.

2. **Talk About It** What is your favorite food? How do you use heating, cooling, and mixing to make it?

Lesson 4

Which Changes Are Not Reversible?

Building Background

Matter can change forms.
Some changes are not reversible.

Inquiry Skill

Observe You can draw pictures to show what you observe.

 STANDARDS

1.b. *Students know* the properties of substances can change when the substances are mixed, cooled, or heated.
4.a. Draw pictures that portray some features of the thing being described.

What You Need

goggles

burned toast

plastic knife

paper and crayons

Burned Toast

Steps

1 **Observe** Look at the toast. Think about how bread looks before it is toasted. **Safety:** Do not taste the bread!

STEP 1

2 **Experiment** Use the knife to scrape off the top layer of the toast. **Safety:** A knife is sharp!

STEP 2

3 **Communicate** Draw a picture of what comes off the bread. Share your observations with a classmate.

STEP 3

Think and Share

1. How did the bread change when it burned?

2. **Infer** Can toast be unburned? Why?

Ask Questions Ask questions to find out what other changes cannot be undone. **Work together** with a partner to find answers.

Vocabulary

reversible change

Reading Skill

Compare and Contrast

Compare	Contrast

STANDARDS

1.b. *Students know* the properties of substances can change when the substances are mixed, cooled, or heated.

Reversible or Not Reversible

A **reversible change** is a change that can be undone. Some changes are reversible, but other changes are not reversible.

This shows a reversible change. Melted ice can be frozen again.

Express Lab

Activity Card 28
Identify a Change That Is Not Reversible

Compare and Contrast How is melting ice different from burning wood?

These show changes that are not reversible. You cannot uncook an egg.

When wood burns, it will stay burned.

Lesson Wrap-Up

❶ **Vocabulary** What is a **reversible change**?

❷ **Reading Skill** How are melting and freezing alike?

❸ **Observe** How can drawing pictures help you understand changes that are not reversible?

💻 **Technology** Visit www.eduplace.com/cascp to find out more about changes that are not reversible.

STANDARDS 1–2: 1.b., 3: 4.a.

Math Salad Mixture

Mr. Abbott's class made fruit salad. This is the recipe they used. Make a bar graph that shows how much of each fruit was used in the salad.

1. Which fruit was used most?

2. How many more bananas than oranges were used?

Fruit Salad
5 apples
4 bananas
3 pears
3 oranges
Wash the apples and pears.
Peel the bananas and oranges.
Chop the fruit. Mix.

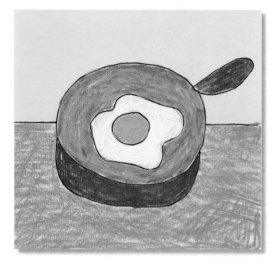

Writing Describe a Change

When have you seen heat change matter? Write a paragraph that tells what happened.

Tara Gomez

What materials make up living things? How do these materials change from day to day? Tara Gomez wants to find answers to these questions.

Ms. Gomez is a biology student in California. For her career, she wants to have her own laboratory.

Visual Summary

Properties can change when matter is heated, cooled, or mixed with other matter. Some changes are reversible.

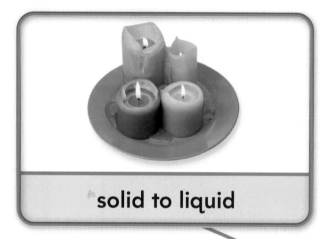

solid to liquid

liquid to solid

Changing Matter

mixing

evaporating

Review your answers to the Lesson Preview questions.

STANDARDS 1.a., 1.b., 3.c.

Main Ideas

1. What does heat from the Sun do? (p. 256)

2. What is a mixture? Explain your answer with an example. (p. 270)

3. Name one change that is reversible. (p. 280)

Vocabulary

Choose the correct word from the box.

4. To change from a liquid to a solid

5. To change from a liquid to a gas

6. To change from a solid to a liquid

7. To mix completely

dissolve (p. 272)
freeze (p. 264)
evaporate (p. 259)
melt (p. 258)

Using Science Skills

8. How can drawing a picture help you explain changes that are reversible?

9. **Critical Thinking** When you toast a marshmallow, is the change reversible? Why?

STANDARDS 1: 3.c, 2–3: 1.b., 4–6: 1.a., 1.b., 7: 1.b., 8: 4.a., 9: 1.b.

Test Practice

Choose the correct answer.

1. Which picture shows a liquid?

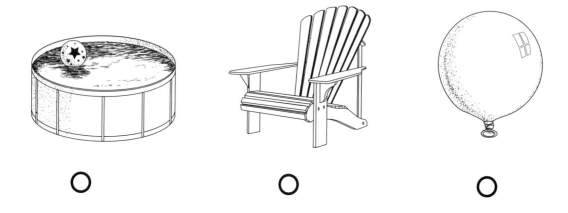

    ○   ○   ○

2. Which form of matter has its own shape?

   solid   liquid   gas
    ○   ○   ○

3. Which form of matter fills all the space it is in?

   solid   liquid   gas
    ○   ○   ○

4. What happens to the water in a puddle when the Sun comes out?

   It melts.   It freezes.   It evaporates.
    ○   ○   ○

5. Earth gets heat from _____.

water   the Sun   reversible
                                       change

  ○   ○   ○

6. Cooling a liquid can change it to _____.

a gas   a mixture   a solid

  ○   ○   ○

Checking Main Ideas

Write the correct answer.

7. Describe what happens when ice is heated.

8. Name a solid, a liquid, and a gas in the fish tank.

STANDARDS 1–3: 1.a., 4: 1.b., 3.c.,
5: 3.c., 6–7: 1.b., 8: 1.a.

287

You Can...

Discover More

Will a pumpkin float in water?

A pumpkin has a large center space filled with air and seeds. The air is a gas that helps the pumpkin float. If you fill that center space with water, the pumpkin will sink a little lower.

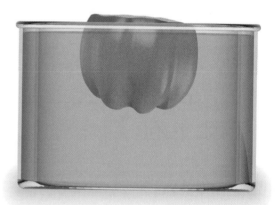

 Simulations Go to **www.eduplace.com/cascp** to test which objects sink and which objects float.

Science and Math Toolbox

Using a Hand Lens

A hand lens is a tool that makes objects look bigger. It helps you see the small parts of an object.

Look at a Coin

1 Place a coin on your desk.

STEP 1

2 Hold the hand lens above the coin. Look through the lens. Slowly move the lens away from the coin. What do you see?

3 Keep moving the lens away until the coin looks blurry.

STEP 3

4 Then slowly move the lens closer. Stop when the coin does not look blurry.

STEP 4

Using a Thermometer

A thermometer is a tool used to measure temperature. Temperature tells how hot or cold something is. It is measured in degrees.

Find the Temperature of Water

1. Put water into a cup.

2. Put a thermometer into the cup.

3. Watch the colored liquid in the thermometer. What do you see?

4. Find the top of the red liquid. What number is next to it? That is the temperature of the water.

Using a Ruler

A ruler is a tool used to measure the length of objects. Rulers measure length in inches or centimeters.

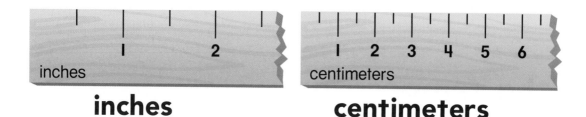

inches   **centimeters**

Measure a Crayon

1 Place the ruler on your desk.

2 Lay your crayon next to the ruler. Line up one end with the end of the ruler.

3 Look at the other end of the crayon. Which number is closest to that end?

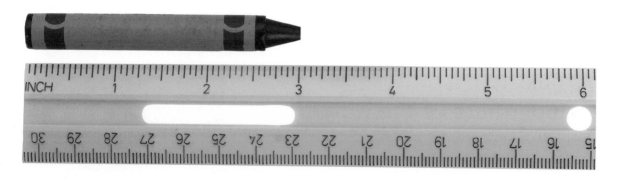

Using a Calculator

A calculator is a tool that can help you add and subtract numbers.

Subtract Numbers

1 Tim and Anna grew plants. Tim grew 5 plants. Anna grew 8 plants.

2 How many more plants did Anna grow? Use your calculator to find out.

3 Enter $\boxed{8}$ on the calculator. Then press the $\boxed{-}$ key. Enter $\boxed{5}$ and press $\boxed{=}$.

What is your answer?

Tim's Plants

Anna's Plants

Using a Balance

A balance is a tool used to measure mass. Mass is the amount of matter in an object.

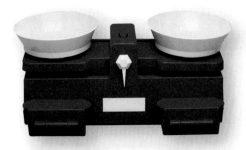

Compare the Mass of Objects

1 Check that the pointer is on the middle mark of the balance. If needed, move the slider on the back to the left or right.

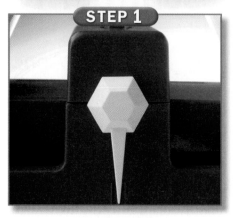
STEP 1

2 Place a clay ball in one pan. Place a crayon in the other pan.

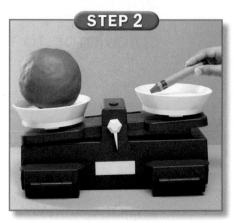
STEP 2

3 Observe the positions of the two pans.

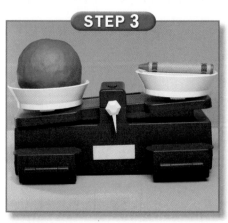
STEP 3

Does the clay ball or the crayon have more mass?

Making a Chart

A chart can help you sort information, or data. When you sort data it is easier to read and compare.

Make a Chart to Compare Animals

1 Give the chart a title.

2 Name the groups that tell about the data you collect. Label the columns with the names.

3 Carefully fill in the data in each column.

Which animal can move in the most ways?

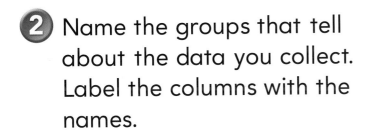

How Animals Move

Animal	How It Moves
fish	swim
dog	walk, swim
duck	walk, fly, swim

Making a Tally Chart

A tally chart helps you keep track of items as you count.

Make a Tally Chart of Kinds of Pets

Jan's class made a tally chart to record the number of each kind of pet they own.

1 Every time they counted one pet, they made one tally.

2 When they got to five, they made the fifth tally a line across the other four.

3 Count the tallies to find each total.

How many of each kind of pet do the children have?

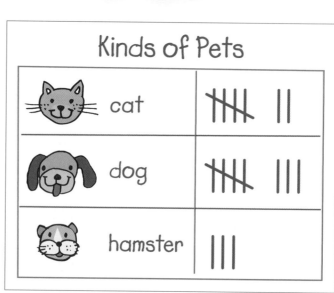

Kinds of Pets

🐱	cat	‖‖‖ ‖
🐶	dog	‖‖‖ ‖‖
🐹	hamster	‖‖

Making a Bar Graph

A bar graph can help you sort and compare data.

Make a Bar Graph of Favorite Pets

You can use the data in the tally chart on page H8 to make a bar graph.

1 Choose a title for your graph.

2 Write numbers along the side.

3 Write pet names along the bottom.

4 Start at the bottom of each column. Fill in one box for each tally.

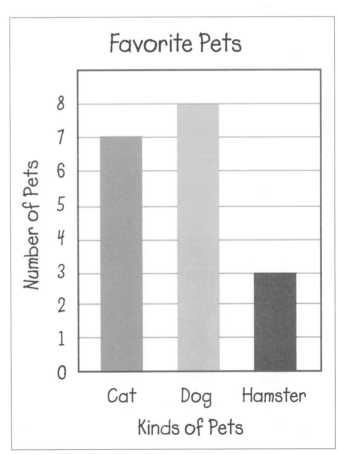

Which pet is the favorite?

Health and Fitness Handbook

Are you healthy? You are if you:

- know how your body works.
- practice safe actions when you play.
- know how to stay well.
- are active every day.
- eat healthful foods.

Inside Your Body

Your body has many parts. All the parts work together.

Brain

Your brain helps you think. It controls all your other body parts.

Lungs

Air goes in and out of your lungs. Your body needs air to stay alive.

Heart

Your heart pumps blood through your body. Your heart is about the size of your fist.

Stomach

Your stomach helps change food so your body can use it.

Bones and muscles hold you up and help you move.

Bones

Your body has more than 200 bones. Some bones protect body parts.

- Your skull protects your brain.

- Your ribs protect your heart and lungs.

- There are 27 bones in each of your hands.

Muscles

Muscles move body parts.

- The muscles in your legs are large. They help you run, jump, and play.

- The muscles in your eyelids are tiny. They help you blink.

- Your heart is a muscle, too.

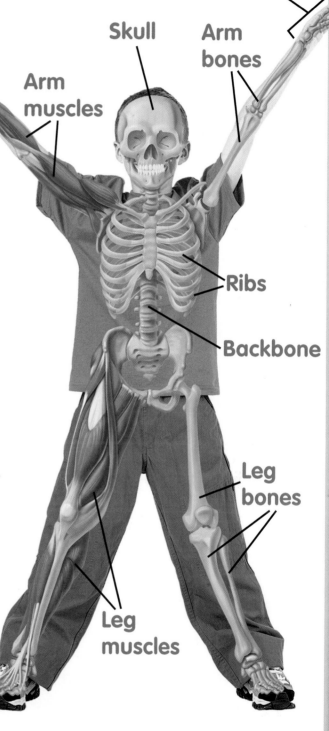

Hand bones

Skull

Arm bones

Arm muscles

Ribs

Backbone

Leg bones

Leg muscles

Foods for Healthy Bones and Teeth

Your body needs calcium. Calcium makes bones and teeth strong. Get the right amount of calcium by eating three of these foods every day!

Dairy Foods

- milk
- yogurt
- cheese

Foods With Calcium Added

- cereal bars
- wheat bread
- cereal
- juices
- tofu
- waffles

Other Foods

- spinach
- bok choy
- garbanzo beans
- almonds

These foods give you one serving of calcium.

calcium-added orange juice

breakfast bar

two burritos

macaroni and cheese

Caring for Your Teeth

You use your teeth to chew, talk, and smile.

Brush Twice Each Day

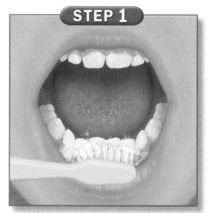
STEP 1
Brush the fronts.

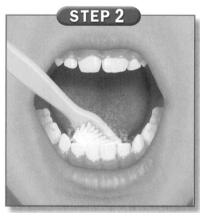
STEP 2
Brush the backs.

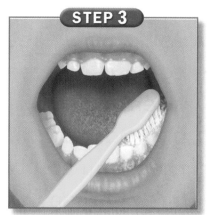
STEP 3
Brush the tops.

Floss Once Each Day

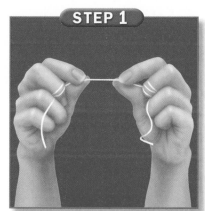
STEP 1
Wrap the floss and pull it tight.

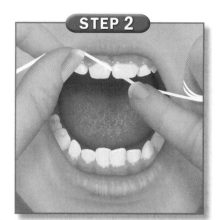
STEP 2
Slide the floss between teeth.

Dental Check-Ups

Dentists and dental hygienists clean and check your teeth. They use x-ray machines to check the hidden parts of teeth.

Fun and Fit on the Playground

Have Some Fun

It's time to go outside. How will you play today? Being active keeps your body fit. You feel good when you are fit. You can play hard and not get tired. You can bend your body in many ways.

Throw, kick, and catch.

Getting and Staying Fit

Do different activities to get fit and stay fit. Stretch before you start. Play hard. Then stretch again. Try these Fun and Fit ideas.

Climb, skip, or swing.

Have fun with friends.

A Safe Bike

You probably know how to ride a bike. Is your bike the right size? Your feet should reach the pedals easily. Your body should be above the bar when you stand.

Safety Equipment

Wear a helmet every time you ride. It should fit flat and protect your forehead. Pull the strap tight.

The right equipment can help keep you safe.

bell

front reflector

rear reflector

reflector

pedal reflectors

English-Spanish

Picture Glossary

coast

A land and water habitat along an ocean. (118)

costa Hábitat formado por tierra y agua a lo largo de un océano.

dissolve

To mix completely. (272)

disolver Mezclar totalmente.

energy

The power to cause change. Energy from the Sun warms land, air, and water. (28, 88, 170, 256)

energía Capacidad de causar cambios. La energía del Sol calienta la tierra, el aire y el agua.

environment

All of the living and nonliving things around a living thing. These fish live in an ocean environment. (82)

medio ambiente Todos los seres vivos y las cosas sin vida que rodean a un ser vivo. El medio ambiente de estos peces es el océano.

evaporate

To change from a liquid to a gas. Heat from the Sun makes puddles evaporate. (259)

evaporar Cambiar de líquido a gas. El calor del Sol hace que los charcos se evaporen.

fall

The season that follows summer. (204)

otoño La estación que sigue al verano.

fins
The body parts a fish uses to move in water. (56)

aletas Las partes del cuerpo con las que un pez se mueve en el agua.

flower
The part of a plant that makes seeds. (19)

flor La parte de una planta que produce semillas.

food chain
The order in which energy moves from one thing to another. (90)

cadena alimenticia El orden en que la energía se mueve de una cosa a otra.

freeze
To change from a liquid to a solid. (264)

helarse Cambiar de líquido a sólido.

G

gas

Matter that spreads out to fill all the space it is in. The balloon is filled with a gas. (242)

gas Materia que se expande hasta rellenar todo el espacio en el que se encuentra. El globo está lleno de gas.

H

habitat

A part of an environment where a plant or an animal lives. (118)

hábitat Parte del medio ambiente donde vive una planta o un animal.

heat

A kind of energy that makes things warm. Heat from a stove warms a room. (256)

calor Tipo de energía que caldea las cosas. El calor de una estufa caldea una habitación.

L

leaves

Parts of a plant that make food for the plant. (19)

hojas Partes de una planta que producen su alimento.

liquid

Matter that flows and takes the shape of its container. (234)

líquido Materia que fluye y toma la forma de su recipiente.

living thing

Something that needs air, food, water, and space to live. Plants and animals are living things. (82)

ser vivo Algo que necesita aire, alimento, agua y un espacio para vivir. Las plantas y los animales son seres vivos.

M

matter

What all things are made of. (226)

materia Elementos de los que están hechas todas las cosas.

meat eater

An animal that eats other animals. A meat eater has sharp teeth. (61)

carnívoro Animal que se come a otros animales. Un carnívoro tiene dientes afilados.

melt

To change from a solid to a liquid. (258)

derretirse Cambiar de sólido a líquido.

mixture

Two or more kinds of matter put together. (270)

mezcla Dos o más tipos de materia que se juntan.

mountain

A high part of Earth's surface. (134)

montaña Parte alta de la superficie de la Tierra.

nonliving thing

Something that does not need food, water, and air to live. Rocks are nonliving things. (82)

cosa sin vida Algo que no necesita alimento, agua o aire para vivir. Las rocas son cosas sin vida.

nutrients

Materials in the soil that plants need to grow. A plant takes in nutrients through its roots. (22)

nutrientes Materiales del suelo que necesitan las plantas para crecer. Una planta toma nutrientes a través de sus raíces.

plant eater

An animal that eats mostly plants. A plant eater has flat teeth. (60)

herbívoro Animal que come mayormente plantas. Un herbívoro tiene dientes planos.

properties

The color, shape, size, and texture of an object. You use your senses to describe an object's properties. (228)

propiedades El color, forma, tamaño y textura de un objeto. Tú utilizas los sentidos para describir las propiedades de un objeto.

reversible change

A change that can be undone. Melting ice is a reversible change because you can freeze it again. (280)

cambio reversible Un cambio que puede modificarse. Derretir hielo es un cambio reversible, porque puedes producir hielo de nuevo.

roots

Parts of a plant that take in water and hold the plant in the ground. (19)

raíces Partes de la planta que toman agua y mantienen a la planta sujeta al suelo.

season

A time of year that has its own kind of weather. (184)

estación Época del año que tiene su propio tiempo.

shadow

What forms when an object blocks light. (172)

sombra Lo que se forma cuando un objeto bloquea la luz.

shelter

A safe place for animals to live. (45, 96)

refugio Lugar seguro donde viven los animales.

soil

The loose top layer of Earth. (22)

tierra La primera capa del suelo de la Tierra.

solid

Matter that has its own size and shape. (226)

sólido Materia que tiene su propia forma y tamaño.

spring

The season that follows winter. Weather begins to get warmer in spring. (190)

primavera Estación que sigue al invierno. El tiempo se vuelve más cálido en la primavera.

stem

The part of a plant that connects the roots to the other plant parts and holds up the plant. (19)

tallo Parte de la planta que conecta las raices con las otras partes de la planta y hace que la planta esté firme.

stream

A small river. (126)

arroyo Río pequeño.

structures

Parts that help plants and animals live in their environments. Hooves help goats walk on rocks. (102)

estructuras Partes que ayudan a las plantas y animales en el medio ambiente. Las pezuñas ayudan a las cabras a caminar por las rocas.

summer

The season that follows spring. Summer is the warmest season. (196)

verano La estación que sigue a la primavera. El verano es la estación más cálida.

sunlight

Light from the Sun. (10)

luz solar Luz que proviene del Sol.

T

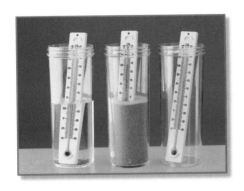

temperature

How warm or cool something is. (162)

temperatura Lo cálido o frío que está una cosa.

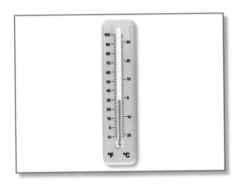

thermometer

A tool that measures temperature. (162)

termómetro Instrumento que mide la temperatura.

W

weather

What the air outside is like. (154)

tiempo Cómo está el aire fuera de la casa.

wind vane

A tool that shows which way the wind blows. (164)

veleta Instrumento que muestra la dirección del viento.

wings

The body parts a bird uses to fly through the air. (57)

alas Parte del cuerpo que un ave utiliza para volar por el aire.

winter

The season that follows fall. (184)

invierno La estación que sigue al otoño.

Credits

Corbis. (pc-tl) © Darrell Gulin/Corbis. (pc-clb) © www.belabaliko.com, 2006. **132–133** (bkgrd) © Royalty-Free/Corbis. **134** (c) Neal Mishler/Getty Images. **134–135** (bkgrd) George Wuerthner. **135** (c) Peter J. Bryant/Biological Photo Service. **136** (tl) © Kevin Schafer/Corbis. **136–137** (bkgrd) Sumio Harada/Minden Pictures. **137** (tr) Bernard Castelein/Nature Picture Library. **139** Jeff Barnard/Associated Press, AP. **140** (t) © Art Wolfe, Inc. (c) Stephen J. Krasemann/DRK Photo. (b) Sumio Harada/Minden Pictures. **144** (l) Franklin Viola/Animals Animals. (c) Maresa Pryor/Animals Animals. (r) G.I. Bernard/Photo Researchers, Inc. Unit C Opener: (bkgrd) Thomas Hallstein/AGE Fotostock. CA Field Trip (tr), (br) Dennis Flaherty Photography.(bkgrd) © Larry Ulrich/DRK Photo. **145** Lionel Isy-Schwart/The Image Bank/Getty Images. **146–147** (bkgrd) © Jon Hicks/Corbis. **148–149** (bkgrd) Tom Till Photography, Inc. **149** (tr) Vito Palmisano/Stone/Getty Images. (br) Philip Coblentz/Brand X Pictures/Getty Images. **150** (t) Promotion Studios. (c) Jeff Grennberg/PhotoEdit, Inc. (b) Bill Boch/Botanica/Getty Images. **150–151** Ariel Skelley. **152** (bl) © HMCo. **152–153** Craig Tuttle/Corbis. **154** (r) Douglas Peebles/Corbis. (l) Ariel Skelley/Corbis. **155** Michael Newman/PhotoEdit, Inc. **156** (tr, cr, br) Cynthia Malaran. **157** Tom Bean/DRK Photo. **160** (bl) Robert Holmes/Corbis. **160–161** Burgess Blevins. **162** Jeff Cadge/The Image Bank/Getty Images. **163** AJA Productions/The Image Bank/Getty Images. **164** (l) David Young-Wolff/Photo Edit, Inc. (r) Jeff Grennberg/PhotoEdit, Inc. **165** (l) David Young-Wolff/PhotoEdit, Inc. (cr) Tony Freeman/PhotoEdit, Inc. **166** (r) © SSPL/The Image Works. **167** (bkgrd) © Jim Steinberg/Animals Animals. **168** (bl) Andersen/Ross/Brand X Pictures/Getty Images. **168–169** (bkgrd) Ingram Publishing/Alamy Images. **170–171** (bkgrd) Trevor Wood/Stone/Getty Images. **172** Bill Boch/Botanica/Getty Images. **173** Thinkstock/Getty Images. **175** (b) Joe Daedele/Getty Images. (b-inset) Tom Pantages Stock Photos. (bkgrd) HO/Reuters/NOAA/Corbis. **176** (c) Jeff Grennberg/PhotoEdit, Inc. (cr) Tony Freeman/PhotoEdit, Inc. (b) Trevor Wood/Getty Images. **178–179** Alan Schein Photography/Corbis. **179** (cl) Chinch Gryniewicz; Ecoscene/Corbis. (cr) Gary Crabbe/Enlightened Images. (bl) Chuck Place/Place Photography. (tr) © Tom Stewart/Corbis. (t) Thomas Mangelsen/Minden Pictures. (c) Photopic/Omni Photo Communications. **180–181** (bkgrd) Dennis Flaherty Photography. **182** (bl) Ariel Skelley/Corbis. **182–183** Stephen St John/National Geographic/Getty Images. **184** (r) Fred Habegger/Grant Heilman Photography. (l) Edward L. Snow/Bruce Coleman, Inc. **185** Thomas Mangelsen/Minden Pictures. **186** (br) Mike Powell/The Image Bank/Getty Images. (bl) Craig C. Sheumaker/Panoramic Images. **187** (cr) Jason Lindsey/Perceptive Visions. **188** (bl) Kim Taylor & Jane Burton/DK Images. **188–189** (bkgrd) Peter Adams Photography/Alamy Images. **190** Photopic/Omni Photo Communications. **191** (bl) Fred Habegger/Grant Heilman Photography. (br) Bill Beatty. (tr) Julie Habel/Corbis. **192** (bl) Robert Glusic/Getty Images. (br) Charles Krebs/Corbis.

193 (cr) Jack Hollingsworth/Getty Images. **194–195** (bkgrd) Goodshot/Alamy Images. **196** Ariel Skelley/Corbis. **197** (bl) Fred Habegger/Grant Heilman Photography. (cr) Harry Rogers/Photo Researchers. (tr) Premium Stock/Corbis. **198** (br) © Thomas Hallstein/outsight.com. (bl) Gibson Stock Photography. **199** (c) © Jeff Greenberg/PhotoEdit, Inc. **200–201** (bkgrd) © Gibson Stock Photography. **201** (t) Diana Koenigsberg/Botanica/Getty Images. (c) Myrleen Ferguson/PhotoEdit, Inc. (b) Michael Newman/PhotoEdit, Inc. **202** (bl) Siede Preis/Photodisc/Getty Images. **202–203** Julio Lopez Saguar/Photonica. **204** Ron Chapple/Thinkstock/Getty Images. **205** (tr) © Dwight Kuhn. (bl) Geoff Bryant/Photo Researchers, Inc. (br) Thase Daniel/Bruce Coleman, Inc. **206** (br) © Ron Niebrugge/Wild Nature Images. (bl) © David Young-Wolff/PhotoEdit, Inc. **207** (cr) Randall B. Henne/Dembinksy Photo Associates. **211** (b) Courtesy of AG Alert/California Farm Bureau Federation. (bkgrd) © Ed Young/Corbis. **212** (br) Ariel Skelley/Corbis. (tr) Jack Hollingsworth/Getty Images. (tl) Thomas Mangelsen/Minden Pictures. (bl) Ron Chapple/Thinkstock/Getty Images. **216** (l) Owaki-Kulla/Corbis. (r) Tony Arruza/Corbis. Unit D Opener: Brad Mitchell/Mira. CA Field Trip (bl) Corbis. (tr), (bkgrd) Gibson Stock Photography. **217** Mark Newman/Lonely Planet Images. **218–219** (bkgrd) Phil Jason/Stone/ Getty Images. **220–221** (bkgrd) Everett Kennedy Brown, Staff/European Pressphoto Agency, EPA/AP Wide World. **221** (tl) Comstock Images/Alamy. (cr) Foodcollection/Alamy Images. **222–223** (bkgrd) ©Imagebroker/Alamy Images. **232–233** (bkgrd) Dynamic Graphics/PictureQuest. **235** (tr) Hanrik Sorensen/Photonica/Getty Images. (b) © Bob Barbour/Minden Pictures. **236** (l) Foodcollection/Alamy Images. (r) Tom Szuba/Masterfile. **237** Micheal Simpson/Taxi/Getty Images. **238** (l) Dr. A.A. Mills. **239** (tr) Kaz Tsuruta/Asian Art Museum. **240** (bl) Raymond Tercafs/Bruce Coleman, Inc. **240–241** (bkgrd) Don Farrall/Photodisc/Getty Images. **242** Michael Venture/Photo Edit, Inc. **247** (inset) © Lynn Davis/Alamy Images. (bkgrd) © Bill Lyons/Alamy Images. **248** (tc) © Bob Barbour/Minden Pictures. (c) Foodcollection/Alamy Images. (bc) Tom Szuba/Masterfile. (tr) Raymond Tercafs/Bruce Coleman, Inc. (br) Michael Venture/PhotoEdit, Inc. **250–251** MedioImages/Getty Images. **251** (cl) Darrell G. Gulin/DRK Photo. (cr) Burke/Triolo Productions/FoodPix/Getty Images. (b) © Coston Stock/Alamy Images. **252** (t) DK Images. **252–253** © Randy Faris/Corbis. **254** (bl) Stephen Shepard/Alamy Images. **254–255** (bkgrd) Pekka, Parviainen/Photo Researchers, Inc. **256** © Cheez/Zefa/Corbis. **257** (bl) Lennox Hearth Products. (tr) Alchemy/Alamy Images. **258** (cr) DK Images. **259** (t, b) Chee Meng Ng Photography. **262** (bl) Michael Newman/PhotoEdit, Inc. **265** (t, b) Stephen G. Maka/DRK Photo. **266** Mark Raycroft/Minden Pictures. **273** Susan Werner/Photographer's Choice/Getty Images. **278** C Squared Studios/Photodisc/Getty Images. **281** (c) Phil Degginger/Alamy Images. (tr) Adrian Bradbury/Getty Images. **283** (inset) Courtesy of Tara Gomez. (bkgrd) Mauro Fermariello/Science Photo Library/Photo Researchers. **284** (br) Chee Meng Ng Photography.

Assignment

CA Standards TOC ©HMCo. **S1** ©HMCo./Richard Hutchings Photography. **S5** ©HMCo. **6** (b), **8**, **9**, **11**, **16**, **17**, **20**, **21**, **26**, **27**, **42**, **43**, **48**, **50**, **53**, **58**, **59** © HMCo./Ken Karp Photography. **81** © HMCo./Lawrence Migdale Photography. **87**, **95** © HMCo./Richard Hutchings Photography. **100** (tr) © HMCo./Silver Editions. (cr), **101** © HMCo./Ken Karp Photography. **106** (inset), **107** (inset) © HMCo./Silver Editions. **116**, **117**, **125**, **133** © HMCo./Richard Hutchings Photography. **152** © HMCo./Silver Editions. **153** © HMCo./Ken Karp Photography. **160** (tr) © HMCo./Ken Karp Photography. (cr, br) © HMCo./Silver Editions. **161**, **166** © HMCo./Ken Karp Photography. **168**, **169** © HMCo./Richard Hutchings Photography. **182** © HMCo./Ken Karp Photography. **182**, **183** © HMCo./Richard Hutchings Photography. **183**, **186–187** © HMCo./Ken Karp Photography. **188** © HMCo./Silver Editions. **189** © HMCo./Richard Hutchings Photography. **192–193**, **194**, **195**, **198–199**, **203** © HMCo./Ken Karp Photography. **221** (bl) Hmco/Richard Hutchings Photography. **222** (t) © HMCo./Silver Editions. (c) © HMCo./Richard Hutchings Photography. (b) © HMCo./Lawrence Migdale Photography. **224**, **225** © HMCo./Richard Hutchings Photography. **226–227** © HMCo./Ken Karp Photography. **228–229** © HMCo./Silver Editions. **233** © HMCo./Richard Hutchings Photography. **234** © HMCo./Ken Karp Photography. **241** © HMCo./Richard Hutchings Photography. **243** © HMCo./Silver Editions. **244**, **245** © HMCo./Lawrence Migdale Photography. **246** © HMCo./Ken Karp Photography. **248**, **251** © HMCo./Silver Editions. **252** © HMCo./Ken Karp Photography. **252** © HMCo./Bud Endress Photography. **254** (tr) © HMCo./Ken Karp Photography. (cr, br) © HMCo./Richard Hutchings Photography. **255** © HMCo./Richard Hutchings Photography. **257** © HMCo./Lawrence Migdale Photography. **258** © HMCo./Ken Karp Photography. **262–263** © HMCo./Richard Hutchings Photography. **264** © HMCo./Ken Karp Photography. **267** © HMCo./Richard Hutchings Photography. **268** (bl), **268–269** (bkgrd) © HMCo./Bud Endress Photography. **269** (t, c, b) Hmco/Richard Hutchings Photography. **270–271** © HMCo./Bud Endress Photography. **272** © HMCo./Ken Karp Photography. **274**, **275**, **276** © HMCo./Ken Karp Photography. **278** © HMCo./Richard Hutchings Photography. **278** © HMCo./Ken Karp Photography. **279** © HMCo./Richard Hutchings Photography. **280**, **284** (tl, tr) © HMCo./Ken Karp Photography. **284** (bl) © HMCo./Bud Endress Photography.

Illustration

CA Standards (tcr) Leland Klanderman. **12** Jeff Wack. **22** Phil Wilson. **30** Wendy Smith. **34** (t) Daniel Del Valle. (b) Jim Kelly. **48** Liz Conrad. **48–51** Liz Conrad. **66** Jim Kelly. **78** (b) © Leland Klanderman. **86** (tr) Ken Batelman/Batelman Illustration. **90–91** (b) © Leland Klanderman. **95** (inset) Jim Kelly. **108** (tr) Daniel Del Valle. (br) Jim Kelly. **110** (tc) Leland Klanderman. **128–129** (bkgrd) Luigi Galante. **138** (r, bl) Jim Kelly. **149**, **162**, **163** Promotion Studios. **174** (t) Robert Schuster. (br) Jim Kelly. **176** (cl) Promotion Studios. **210** Daniel Del Valle. **224–225** Tim

H39